WAITING FOR THE 5:05

WAITING FOR THE 5:05

TERMINAL, STATION AND DEPOT IN AMERICA

COMPILED BY LAWRENCE GROW

Introduction by Clay Lancaster

Main Street/Universe Books, New York

CONTENTS

Foreword

Introduction by Clay Lancaster

The 5:05 headed west from the massive Chicago and North Western station each week day. Its first stop, some thirty-five miles from the railroad capital of America, was Geneva, and here several hundred commuters eagerly escaped from the rigors of business. But this was not the end of the day for the 5:05. It continued on along the Galena Division, dropping off packages for small town merchants, empty mail sacks and milk cans at rural flag-stops, and the remaining passengers. The end of the trip for the train's crew came only on the other side of the Mississippi, in Clinton, Iowa, 138 miles from Chicago. It was not a very exciting or romantic excursion, but, then, in the 1940s, it seemed the natural way to travel. For the average American, wherever he lived, going down to the station to meet or catch a train —interurban, suburban, or long-distance— was then as customary as heading for the freeway is now.

Waiting was part of the routine, for if a train departed on schedule, which was rare, it almost never arrived on time. But there were the stations—at each end of the trip— and these were true community centers. One could eat and sometimes sleep and bathe there, and, in some magnificent temples of rail transportation, there were movies to be enjoyed. Few of us thought very much of the stations then. Most were rather grimy, sad places. Now, only when many of them have disappeared from the centers of towns and cities, victims of the wrecker's ball, do we begin to understand their real and symbolic worth. Frost and Granger's early twentieth-century station set apart from others in the

area by six massive Doric columns, still stands in Chicago, but has been modernized in a less than felicitous manner by a well-meaning Chicago and North Western management; in little Geneva, the low-lying Richardsonian-style stone depot has been leveled and replaced by a nondescript box. The story is sadly similar elsewhere.

As Clay Lancaster notes in his Introduction which follows, the historical importance of the railroad station is more than the sum of its architectural forms. A vast majority of buildings were designed by engineers rather than architects, and as the reader of this book will discover, stations of exactly the same form and decorative elements were virtually mass-produced by the railroad companies. Most of the trains that arrived and departed were not of the glamorous sort nostalgically recalled today—the Twentieth Century Limited, the Burlington Zephyrs, the Wabash Blue Bird. The majority of trains carried passengers, whether daily commuters or not, for only relatively short distances. Most of the stations that were used were usually modest structures, however distinguished their design. The importance ascribed to them and the interest displayed in them today is a reflection of our concern for the loss of a meaningful community institution.

In Lancaster's words, "The train station was the image of the community, presenting at a glance something about its size, affluence, livelihood and social range of its citizens, their taste in architecture. . . . The railroad depot is the foremost symbol of the evolving period of American civilization, of which there has been no replacement." Nor does there seem to be any real prospect that the station will again play any important role. Rail transportation is on the comeback trail, but the stations of the past, if saved at all, are more likely to be used as restaurants and cultural centers. Because of their central geographic and historical position in the community and usually ample physical dimensions, more and more stations are being recycled. Hopefully, this trend will continue.

Still, for those of us born before the jet age, it is difficult to deny memories of real railroading—of listening to the long whistle and rumbling of cars crossing a high iron viaduct, of winding across a labyrinth of switches and tracks to arrive in the terminal of a new city, of gazing up at the play of light and shadow in the seemingly endless expanse of iron and stone which defines so many urban terminals. And if we do appreciate good architectural design, there can be no denying what was an impressive record.

The Historic American Buildings Survey has attempted to document this record since the 1930s. An archival service of the National Park Service, its aim is simply "preservation through documentation," and this is achieved by means of measured drawings, photographs, and the recording of architectural and historical data at thousands of sites across the country. Traveling exhibitions of photographs and drawings further spread the work of this governmental agency to the general public. *Waiting for the 5:05* is based on such a show, "Terminal, Station and Depot in America," which began a nationwide tour in the fall of 1976 under the auspices of the Smithsonian Institution Traveling Exhibition Service. By the fall of 1978, the show will have been seen in fifteen cities.

The majority of illustrations in this book have been drawn from material prepared for the exhibition by HABS and its sister archival service, the Historic American Engineering Record. Some changes in organization of materials have been made, however, and the number of illustrations increased. A last section of the book is devoted to a sampling of Canadian stations, a chapter in railroading history closely linked with that of the United States.

In compiling all of this material, Mary Farrell, HABS exhibitions coordinator, has been of inestimable assistance. She and John M. Poppeliers, chief of HABS, have generously shared their expertise and resources. Other individuals who have greatly aided the search for accurate and informative material are Eric Delony, principal architect of the Historic American Engineering Record; Robert M. Vogel, curator, Division of Mechanical and Civil Engineering, Museum of History and Technology, Smithsonian Institution; and the following private collectors of railroadiana: H. H. Harwood, Jr., Barton K. Battaile, Dr. Wendell H. McChord, Norton D. Clark, and Dudley H. Brumbach.

Lawrence Grow
March 1977

Editorial note—The following abbreviations are used in the credit lines of illustrations for the sake of brevity:

HABS = Historic American Buildings Survey
HAER = Historic American Engineering Record

Broadly considered, the railroad station was the focus of the American community from the middle of the nineteenth to the middle of the twentieth century. Whether in the populous city on the East or West Coast, Great Lakes or inland waterways, or in the small town or village of New England, the South or on the prairie, the train depot occupied the central position. In the city it could be distinguished by the bustle and activity surrounding it, and it was the one place in the grim metropolis where the inhabitants unleashed their emotions publicly, at the meeting with or separation from loved ones. In smaller settlements it was where the natives congregated to get news and swap gossip, and scrutinize arriving and departing passengers, as bringing a welcome, wider vista to their limited, humdrum existence. The train station was the image of the community, presenting at a glance something about its size, affluence, livelihood, and social range of the citizens, their taste in architecture, and even when their local pride last came to fruition, in the building of the depot. The steamboat landing before it and the airport afterward were located on the edge or outside of the population area; but the tracks of the train were brought to the nucleus, wending their way through the streets of the hamlet or small city, and taken underground in the great metropolis. The architecture of the depot ranged from a shelter, usually slightly more pretentious and up-to-date than the courthouse or town hall of the village, to the magnificence of a temple or palace in the capitals of wealth, industry, and learning. Today the city expands in an aggregate manner, its buildings lacking style and distinction, an aimless continuity of construction without source and without conclusion. This throws into sharper perspective the role that the railroad station played in unifying, in giving a core to American communities maintaining individuality and local character prior to the decline of the railroads. The iron rails and the trains that shuttled from one to another tied them together, but to each place the railroad terminal was its hallmark, standing for all of the cultural, productive, and commercial facets of which the people were capable. The railroad depot is the foremost symbol of the evolving period of American civilization, of which there has been no replacement.

Sparked off by the trial run of Peter Cooper's experimental engine *Tom Thumb* in Maryland, during the fall of 1829, the railroad spread like wildfire throughout the United States. Among the earliest commercial systems were the Baltimore and Ohio, and the South Carolina Railroad. In 1833, when the tracks of the latter extended from Charleston to Hamburg—a distance of 135 miles—it was the longest line in the world. By this time there were railways in Pennsylvania and New York, where the steam-powered rail cars went into competition with the canal system previously undertaken to connect the Great Lakes region with the Atlantic seaboard. The mechanized means soon proved superior to horse-towed canal boats restricted in their movements to level channels. The railroad had the mobility of that other established mode of public conveyance in America, the horse-drawn stagecoach; but it had the advantage of being faster, more reliable, of handling greater volume of traffic, and of being virtually indefatigable. The train played an important role in the development of this vast and varied continent. The series of small and independent train lines which had come into existence east of the Mississippi by the mid-1830s, began to be replaced by more ambitious undertakings. This expansion culminated in the girding of the nation by steel bands in the Golden Spike Ceremony at Promontory Point, Utah, with the joining of the railheads of the Union Pacific and Central Pacific on 10 May 1869. Occurring only a few years after the expiration of the conflict that separated North and South, the completion of the transcontinental railroad was the physical meeting of East and West and consummated the tying together of the four extremities of the Republic.

During that century, beginning when the United States attained its continental breadth (California was admitted as a state in 1850), the railroad was the motif of America. In cities, widespread train yards were a certain indication of a thriving business in trade and transportation. Guy lines from these webs radiating outward coursed through the suburbs, threaded their way along the valleys by meandering streams, climbed the mountains, plunged through towering hills, and laid straight across the plains. Like an arrow sped the overland train, its locomotive head trailing a telltale plume of jet, if a freight its tail a crimson caboose, if a passenger, at night its coaches glowing like lantern fish deep in the nocturnal sea. The whistle echoed far and wide across the landscape, and ranger and farmer judged the time by the scheduled runs. The train brought newcomers, provisions, and merchandise, on which depended the settlement's growth, sustenance, and the amenities of existence; and it carried off local products to the teeming cities that bought and processed them for the world to use. Undercurrent to the great transcontinental systems were the multiplicity of smaller lines, of which many were literally small, operating on tracks of three or even two-foot gauge, long after the official adoption of the English standard of 4 feet 8½ inches following the Civil War. The short runs carried the dairy's milk, the orchard's fruit, the plantation's cotton, and, of course, commuters from outlying residences to their work in the big city. The engine's bell warned of the train's approach to a crossing and, with the whistle, the hour of departure. It had its forefinger on the pulse of America, that neighing of the iron horse.

American railroading was modeled on earlier developments in the Old World. Rail cars, manually- and later horse-propelled, were used for mining in Central Europe at least by the mid-sixteenth century. Newcomen and Watts having shown the practicality of the piston engine for stationary work during the 1760s, a Frenchman, Nicolas Cugnot, soon adapted it to a self-powered vehicle, which got its inventor into trouble by butting into a wall. To avoid this sort of accident the machine was considered safer directed on tracks, and, shortly after the advent of the nineteenth century, Richard Trevithick made the archetypal railroad, which ran along an iron-flanged tramroad at Penydarran in

South Wales. Trevithick's engine was improved by George Stephenson, whose *Locomotive* was the first to work a steam-drawn public railroad, the Stockton and Darling, in 1825. As has been noted, Peter Cooper's *Tom Thumb* succeeded the English vehicle four years later. The form of early American engines followed those across the Atlantic, but within a score of years they displayed independent characteristics. The basic type adopted was that of Englishman Edward Bury, from whom specimens were imported to the United States during the 1830s. Due to a certain kind of firebox with a steam dome above, his was a light engine. It was simplified by the Norris Brothers of Philadelphia, who mounted the cylinders outside; and sympathetic to sharper curves on American lines, they devised a bogie or pivotal truck under the fore part. As this was the time when bison ranged the open lands, a cowcatcher was affixed to the front end. With flaring funnel to decrease the danger of sparks to dry-wooded, brush, and grass areas, and a sheltering cab for the engineer, the look of the American engine was established. Carriages in the United States, as across the sea, originally were modeled after stagecoaches; but American trains soon abandoned doors to individual compartments in favor of entrances in end vestibules. The device stabilized the temperature for passengers, which betokens a low tolerance in the American demand for comfort.

Counterpart to the rolling stock and an indispensable part of the system were railroad stations. At first indistinguishable from other buildings, the train depot came to be a unique type of American architecture. The oldest railroad station in the United States is the

Lexington and Ohio Railroad (Louisville and Nashville) Station, Lexington, Kentucky.
The third story was added c. 1851. Courtesy, Clay Lancaster.

Mount Clare (p. 27) at Baltimore. Built of brick in 1830, it is a compact, polygonal building that has been likened to a toll booth on an early turnpike. This building and neighboring shops and roundhouse have become the B&O/C&O Railroad Museum. The Lexington and Ohio Railroad in Central Kentucky, put into operation in 1832, early used space in the market house for its Lexington terminal. Three years later it engaged twenty-three-year-old John McMurtry to erect a two-story brick structure in the next block east for the purpose. It was a long, narrow building with a series of doors on the lower floor facing the tracks, eminently suited to serving a chain of cars. Replaced by a grand successor (to be referred to later), the old Lexington station was razed for a parking lot in 1959.

The feature that was to set railroad stations apart from other buildings was the covered platform. A. J. Downing said in *Cottage Residences,* published in 1842, that the elements characterizing dwelling houses were chimneys and porches. It was about this time that the latter was modified into the railroad shelter to protect those boarding or debarking from trains. The bracketed veranda, introduced in the Downing book and popularized along with deep overhanging eaves in his *Architecture of Country Houses* of 1850 (in the Swiss chalet and its derivative, his

American farm house) set the style for country stops throughout the United States. The covered platform was magnified to the train shed, sheltering train as well as patrons on the platform. Stripped to bare structural essentials, it became what in this collection is called the train barn. In time it was enormously enlarged and—taking its cue from the Crystal Palace at London of 1851 and later American exhibition halls of similar kind, beginning with that at New York in 1853—it became the great iron and glass concourse of which a milestone was that of old Grand Central Depot (p. 36), erected in New York City in 1869-70. Like the conservatory halls of world's fairs in this country, such as the Philadelphia Centennial of 1876 and Chicago Columbia Exhibition of 1894, the glass train shed was hidden behind a basilica-like exterior that was considered the proper façade for any structure of edifice pretentions.

The railroad was incepted and matured before World War I, when style was the prerequisite for architecture. Its examples embodied the full range of period fashions taken up elsewhere in American building. The Mont Clare and Lexington stations, previously mentioned, were in the Federal style, albeit reduced to the barest elements in window and door frames and projecting cornices. The railroad building was not yet ready to

Illustrations from *Architecture of Country Houses.*
A. J. Downing, 1850.

Utica, 1850, birdseye view, Lewis Bradley.
The station serving the Utica and Schenectady and the Utica and Syracuse railroads is seen to the left of the square. Courtesy, Oneida Historical Society.

assume the monumental extremes of the style, such as were embodied in Thornton's Capitol at Washington, Bulfinch's State House at Boston, and Jefferson's University of Virginia at Charlottesville. It was for the Greek Revival, with its simpler and bolder forms, produced by late technically-improved means, to embellish a building as newly-devised as a depot. This is shown in the railroad station built during the 1840s on Baggs Square in Utica, New York. The station proper had a pedimented tetrastyle facade, flanked on either side by pierced galleries supporting a screen parapet—that on one side being the train shed with a practically flat roof. Atop the main pavilion was a square cupola with corner pilasters capped by an entablature and pediment, an architectural

conceit here, but it may have housed an alarm bell for town purposes.

About contemporary with the Greek was the Gothic Revival, which was foremost of the Romantic styles before the Civil War. In this it seemed patently suited to railroad architecture, as the train was a migratory entity, a link with remote places. The prime models of the Gothic—cathedrals and castles —served uses too far removed from that of catching trains for application to railroad stations, whereas derivatives proved otherwise. Richard Upjohn devised a type of country church sheathed in vertical boards in his *Rural Architecture* of 1852 that provided a satisfactory prototype. Omitting the belfry and perhaps lowering the slope of the roof did not make it less of a trackside ornament.

It made an appropriate suburban depot, like that at Bernardston, Massachusetts, on the Connecticut Valley branch of the Boston and Maine Railroad. At one end a pair of Tudor arches spanned the front of a shallow recess containing an outdoor waiting bench. An oriel window—reduced to an ordinary American bay—projecting on the platform allowed the station master an unobstructed view of the tracks in both directions, and it served as a ticket booth during balmy weather.

Upjohn-inspired Carpenter's Gothic had traits in common with Downing's Swiss chalet and American farmhouse variation, both being of wood and having overhanging eaves requiring supports that were the obvious element to become decorative. The bracketed mode led to a building type with exposed crisscrossing of timbers that has been labeled the Stick Style. Inherent to it was a species of decoration that was flat and an abstraction of floral shapes, generally associated with the name of Charles Locke Eastlake, who wrote articles and books on architecture and household objects in England during the 1860s and early '70s. Eastlake designs were readily cut out of a thin plank by a jigsaw. The torturing of wood by this instrument and the turning lathe led to a multiplicity of new creations too amorphous to be alluded to by any designation other than "gingerbread." It became a sort of folk architecture, and late nineteenth-century country railroad stations were among its most enthusiastic adherents. The Centennial Depot of the Philadelphia and Reading Rail-

road is one such exuberant expression of rustic taste.

In opposition to this anomalous building practice was the identifiable and sophisticated edifice of more affluent communities during the mature period of railroading. A style widely exploited during the middle of the nineteenth century was the Italianate. While retaining the basic orders of the Federal and Greek Revival, the Italianate assumed round arches and arcades, wide eaves and low-pitched roofs, tall towers and chimney stacks, and a picturesque way of massing that was not unlike the Gothic. The Calvert Station (p. 45), built at Baltimore during 1848-50, exemplifies the mode. A vastly larger contemporary, labeled "Italian" at the time it was built, was the depot at New Haven, Connecticut. It was composed largely of arched galleries along the street, connecting a central motif, having hovering roofs as of a Nepalese pagoda, with towers stationed 300 feet apart at the extremities, one resembling a pointed Burmese dagoba, and the other soaring 140 feet into the air and sporting an Indian chaitya arch on four sides below the summit kiosk. The architect was Henry Austin, whose forms were often confusing whether Mediterranean or Dravidian in origin.

By mid-century the pure or simple hybrid Revivals of the preceding decades were being replaced by Eclecticism, whose sources were complex, whose elements resulted from a combination of styles, and they were further complicated by a sprinkling of innovations. Thus the persisting Classic, which had manifested a limited number of plain Roman and Greek motifs earlier, became the Renaissance Revival during the latter half of the nineteenth century, a double reversion to the original phenomenon, as the European Renaissance of the fifteenth century onward had been a reflection of antiquity. The design of the five-pavilion complex forming the south front of old Grand Central Depot in New York (p. 36) stressed vertical and horizontal edges by quoins and entablatures, accentuated openings by porticoes, pilasters and consoled pediment hoods, and crowned masses with parapets and balustrades surmounted by mansard roofs, making as much architectonic fuss over the façade as the iron-and-glass train shed behind was emancipated from this sort of thing. The mood was that of constant agitation, allowing the eye no blank space upon which to rest. Even the summit of the roofs, the only notable surfaces not pierced by fenestration, curved inward by way of circumventing plainness.

The Gothic inheritance of consequence during the latter half of the nineteenth century turned away from English sources, which had been its mainstay before the Civil War, to Continental European manifestations. Greatly influential were two books by John Ruskin, *The Seven Lamps of Architecture* and *Stones of Venice,* published simultaneously at New York and London in 1849 and 1851, though the latter volume in its entirety did not appear in America until 1860. Due to its sea trade, Venice was the most Oriental city in Europe, its architecture contrasting to the gray stone buildings of northern countries in displaying polychromy in its masonry and great richness of decoration. The upward thrust of northern Gothic—in soaring piers, lancet arches, and steep roofs—was supplanted on the Mediterranean by an equal amount of recumbent elements and lower-pitched openings and coverings. The Victorian Gothic style in the United States also incorporated features from other European countries. A good example of post-Civil War Gothic is the station at Point of Rocks, Maryland (p. 54). It has walls of red brick, granite, and sandstone, and roof of slate. The checkerboard motif is accomplished by horizontal banding across upright forms, with voussoirs of alternating colors arching the principal windows, and half dormers pushing up through the long eaves. Plan and wall contours shift, and the roof changes slope and varies between hip and gable with ridge.

The principle of faceting forms and articulating surfaces to extremes applies equally to all phases of Eclecticism. It provides a clue for recognizing the period, by overriding the style source of elements, which remain incidental to effect. In many buildings, such as Frank Furness's B. & O. Station in Philadelphia (pp. 69 - 70), the origin of the parts remain obscure. They are neither Renaissance nor Venetian Gothic, nor can they be fitted under any other label; they are examples of Creative Eclecticism.

Eclecticism of a special category derived from that other medieval style preceding Gothic, the Romanesque. Although the Romanesque appeared sporadically during the Revival era—as in Richard Upjohn's Church of the Pilgrims (1844) on Brooklyn Heights, New York City, and in the sketches for a Norman villa (Design XX) in Downing's *Country Houses* —it remained for Henry Hobson Richardson to popularize it, largely due to the admiration accrued from his Trinity Church (1874) in Boston, inspired by the old cathedral at Salamanca in Spain. Richardson was not so historically influenced in designs for lesser buildings, as shown in the stone station at North Easton, Massachusetts (p. 64), which is typical of his style. We are struck by a certain bigness of form, a bold handling of blocks of sandstone and granite, and a sculpturesque undulation of shingled surfaces, altogether a very personal treatment. Both types of his work begot progeny in America, the latter in all sorts of buildings in suburbia, and the former in impressive public buildings, courthouses, post offices, and railroad stations heading the list. Richard Montfort's Union Station in Nashville (pp. 76 - 78) is a good illustration, a facsimile in massing of the master's Allegheny County Court House and Jail in Pittsburgh. Conspicuous are semicircular arches

North Station, Boston, Massachusetts.
Courtesy, Norton D. Clark.

16

on squat colonnettes and featuring ample, smooth archivolts, a foil to rough stonework elsewhere, with limestone mullions crossing the larger windows, and cylindrical corner buttresses capped by conical-roofed turrets, the composition attaining climax in the square central tower. Union stations at Louisville (1880-91) and St. Louis (1894) are in the same manner (pp. 79 - 83).

The tendency shown in larger buildings to adhere to orthodox styles culminated in the monumental examples of the early twentieth century. Stimulated by the Neo-Classic architecture of gigantic proportions at the world's fairs at Chicago in 1894 and Saint Louis ten years later, these structures presented overwhelming triumphal arches, colonnades, and vaulted and domed interiors, fabricated largely of fine-grained white mar-ble. Many of them sprawled over an entire city block. Outstanding examples are Daniel H. Burnham's Union Station in Washington, D.C. (1906), McKim, Mead and White's Pennsylvania Station (1906-10), and Whitney Warren and others' Grand Central Terminal (1903-12) in New York City (pp. 113 - 116). Burnham was head architect for the World's Columbian Exposition and his Washington Station bears a strong resemblance to the Terminal at the Chicago fair (p. 110). The spacious barrel-vaulted waiting room, measuring 130 by 200 feet, opens up at either end to a ticket lobby and dining room of similar shape and half size. The splendid waiting room of New York's Pennsylvania Station was derived from the Baths of Caracalla, whereas the concourse was an engineer's exercise in steel lattice supports

Union Depot, Lexington, Kentucky.
Courtesy, Dr. Wendell H. McChord.

and glass arches. Its pillared exterior was more overpowering than any Roman forum. Grand Central's façade of coupled fluted columns and sculptured Mercury group by Jules-Alexis Coutan has gained genuine public approval, which is called on periodically to save it from the fate that befell Pennsylvania station. Lesser exponents of Neo-Classic include that contemporary to the planning period of the Chicago fair, the North Station (1893) at Boston and John Russell Pope's Broad Street Station in Richmond (1919) (p. 117). Another example is Richards, McCarty and Bulford's Union Station (1907) in Lexington, Kentucky, a building of yellow brick and colored glass that replaced the 1835 depot and itself was destroyed in 1960.

Medium-sized stations in Neo-Classic garb appeared second-rate in comparison to the capacious edifices, and the casual modes fell short of the impression it was wished for them to make. A worthy pattern for such buildings was the Spanish. Like the Italianate earlier, the range of the Iberian style extended from a verbatim European Renaissance-Baroque to a basic provincial, in this case Spanish Colonial, taken from mission churches and adobe ranchos in our own Southwest. The last was publicized through the complex erected for the California-Pacific Exposition at San Diego in 1915 (p. 91) to celebrate the opening of the Panama Canal. The two extremes, as applied to railroad stations, are shown in specimens dating from 1915. The sophisticated Union Station at Worcester, Mass., is built of white marble and has a center pavilion beholden to the monumental style. Flanking it were identical towers in the Churrigueresque manner, building up by stages from a rusticated square base to diminishing octagons

Union Station, Worcester, Massachusetts.
Courtesy, Herbert H. Harwood, Jr.

New York, New Haven, and Hartford Railroad Station, Waterbury, Connecticut.
Courtesy, Herbert H. Harwood, Jr.

Terminal Station, Chattanooga, Tennessee.
Chattanooga Choo Choo Co.
Courtesy, Chattanooga, Choo Choo Co.

ending in points 175 feet above the pavement. Its main waiting room is a small version of that at Washington. The simple colonial type is represented, significantly, by the station at San Diego. The building is as stark as its prototype of the padres, with a low, continuous stucco arcade along the street showing a clerestory above and back of its tiled roof, terminating in a single unpretentious tower with an arch on each of two levels, the upper crowned by a dome and cupola.

The foregoing paragraphs touch on the high points of the architectural styles affecting railroad stations through the first quarter of the twentieth century. During the score of years afterward, or until the unforeseen decline of the railroad, stations continued to be built. One of the most impressive was Union Terminal in the northwest quarter of Cincinnati (p. 121). It was opened in 1933 and was of contemporary design, as geometric as the exhibition buildings at the Century of Progress fair in Chicago of that year. A vast axial layout of roadways led up to the great glass arch that was façade to the semispherical main hall. During its heyday the station accommodated 17,000 travelers and 216 trains daily.

Railroad depots occasionally have housed restaurants and other inn facilities, shops, and enterprises further removed from its transportation objective, but on the whole the station has remained a distinct species of American building. It is perhaps ironic that when it attained to pure functionalism in design, as in the Cinicinnati terminal, the function of the railroads it served was starting on the downgrade. The wrecking ball and bulldozer showed no mercy, not only to stations that were deprived entirely of their original purpose, but to those whose site was at a commercial premium. Pennsylvania Station in New York is one so ill-fated: its magnificence was swept away for a games arena (confusedly called Madison Square Garden) and office tower, with train service permitted an anonymous existence underground. Some stations found other uses, such as that with the graceful Romanesque campanile (1908) at Waterbury, Connecticut, which became a newspaper office in 1952. Another is the terminal (1909) at Chattanooga, Tennessee, whose waiting room was converted into a 1,300-place restaurant, and another part into a caravanserai, with train coaches becoming family suites (two to a car) in 1973. In the United States the locomotive's bell and whistle now have become an echo that has all but died out. The station has shared the train's fate. They both may be contemplated in retrospect, though not justifiably without a nostalgic tribute to a noble era of prodigious achievements.

Almost until the mid-twentieth century and the building of an interstate highway system, rail transportation and its course of development has paralleled that of America's social and economic progress as a nation. First, of course, there were the frontier trails and waterways, each of which followed the most natural geographic routes. Then, in the East, came the first man-made canals which served to link nature technologically with European-style civilization. By the 1830s small rail lines, tentative feelers, were beginning to inch out from such urban centers as Boston, New York, Baltimore, and Charleston. In 1869, when transcontinental travel first became possible, the network of lines had begun to assume the form of a cobweb. From then on each step in industrial and agricultural technology was matched by a further extension of the railroad as well as by population growth. European immigrants followed the lines to the West; French-Canadians traveled south to New York state and New England; African-Americans moved north in search of new lives. Until the gas combustion engine started to disseise mountains and streams, neighborhoods and center cities, the railroad was the *way* to mobility and progress.

As with any great change in technology, as Ralph Waldo Emerson reminds us, the first advances were viewed as a mixed blessing:

> I hear the whistle of the locomotive in the woods. Wherever that music comes it has its sequel. It is the voice of the civility of the Nineteenth Century saying, "Here I am."

But more quickly than most people, Americans began accepting and defining their new railroad age and all of its accoutrements.

Railroad map of the United States, 1870.
By this time the national network of rail lines numbered 52,992 miles.
The Union Pacific and Central Pacific (Southern Pacific) western route, branching out from
Council Bluffs, Iowa, is shown running through Federal land grants which, in part,
paralleled the old Mormon, Oregon, and California trails.
The Association of American Railroads.

The trial run of the Tom Thumb between Baltimore and Ellicott City (Ellicott Mills), Maryland, 1830.

The Lackawanna Valley by George Innes, 1855.
*Innes was commissioned by the Delaware, Lackawanna and Western Railroad (Erie Lackawanna)
to paint picturesque landscapes of the company's northeast Pennsylvania territory.
Scranton's impressive roundhouse is clearly visible in the background.
Innes and other important artists also supplied sketches which were used in
railroad travel guides and brochures.
National Gallery of Art, Washington, D.C.*

MOTHERS LOOK OUT FOR YOUR CHILDREN!
ARTISANS, MECHANICS, CITIZENS!

When you leave your family in health, must you be hurried home to mourn a

DREADFUL CASUALITY!

PHILADELPHIANS, your RIGHTS are being invaded! regardless of your interests, or the LIVES OF YOUR LITTLE ONES. THE CAMDEN AND AMBOY, with the assistance of other companies without a Charter, and in VIOLATION OF LAW, as decreed by your Courts, are laying a

LOCOMOTIVE RAIL ROAD!

Through your most Beautiful Streets, to the RUIN of your TRADE, annihilation of your RIGHTS, and regardless of your PROSPERITY and COMFORT. **Will you permit this!** or do you consent to be a

SUBURB OF NEW YORK!!

Rails are now being laid on BROAD STREET to CONNECT the TRENTON RAIL ROAD with the WILMINGTON and BALTIMORE ROAD, under the pretence of constructing a City Passenger Railway from the Navy Yard to Fairmount!!! This is done under the auspices of the CAMDEN AND AMBOY MONOPOLY!

RALLY PEOPLE in the Majesty of your Strength and forbid THIS

OUTRAGE!

An 1839 poster announcing the imminent threat of the Camden and Amboy
Railroad's rail line down Philadelphia's Broad Street to link the Trenton and Wilmington/Baltimore lines.
Safety rarely came first in such early projects, and considerable political conniving
was necessary to effect their approval.
Union Pacific Railroad Museum Collection.

"This is the crowd that met me when I came to Rockport, Tex." Postcard, c. 1910. What better way to arrive in this sunny Gulf Coast town, situated on a branch line of the Southern Pacific? The passenger depot was still a major center of community life and something to write home about.
Library of Congress.

Across the Continent, Currier and Ives, 1868.
The romance and excitement of a transcontinental train trip is fully captured in this popular engraving.
The first three cars carry the legend "Through Line/New York/San Francisco Co."
Such a journey, however, could not have been made completely by rail until the following year, 1869.
The engraving is based on Emanuel Leutze's Westward the Course of Empire.
Library of Congress.

As the needs of the railroad and its customers developed over the years, so did the form of the station. Little attention was at first given to building any sort of mighty edifice; the majority of stations were probably hastily converted homes, hotels, or inns. The series of drawings included in this section illustrates the basic progression from a simple one-sided station to the head form with side wings and an elaborate shed. Technology in large part kept pace with the railroad companies' demands, although in other respects, such as comfort, America lagged behind England. An early historian of American transportation, John Luther Ringwalt, wrote as late as the 1880s that stations "were as a rule, conspicuous by the absence of the accommodation and convenience which characterize the stations on English or continental railways . . . little more than rough sheds giving shelter. . . ." But for all that America lacked in the niceties of travel, it made up in originality of architectural expression—from Greek Revival to the Italianate railroad style and Gothic Revival to other and increasingly eclectic fashions, Romanesque Revival, Shingle Style, Spanish Colonial, Beaux Arts. Such an expansive nation seemed to have room for every idiosyncratic "revival." Only when the railroads themselves were hitting the skids in the 1930s did the rush of creativity falter and finally die.

Baltimore and Ohio Station, Frederick, Maryland, 1831.
Tracks still ran into this early station when a photographer chanced across it around 1906.
It is most representative of the structures which served the needs of the railroads
and their customers in the first decades of operation.
Library of Congress.

Mt. Clare Station,
Baltimore and Ohio Railroad,
Baltimore, Maryland, 1830.
*America's oldest surviving station,
Mt. Clare is now the home of the
B. & O. Transportation Museum.
Late Georgian in style, it was built
in polygonal form and originally served as
nothing more than a ticket office.
E. H. Pickering, HABS, 1936.*

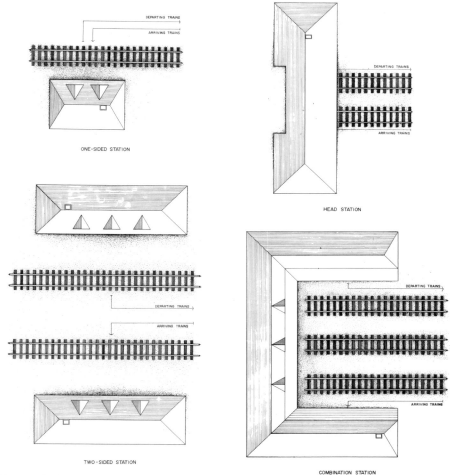

ONE-SIDED STATION

HEAD STATION

TWO-SIDED STATION

COMBINATION STATION

*The evolution of the station is sketched from the one-sided to the combination.
The earliest and simple one-sided form is most commonly found today in suburban and country
locations; the two-sided, of course, allowed for increased traffic and safety. The head station form
was introduced in the mid-nineteenth century and became the predominant one for
town and city terminals and depots. Expanded with side wings as a combination freight and passenger station,
the head form provided the American metropolis with an imposing, if not monumental, public building.
Pamela Chang, HABS, 1975.*

VIEW OF ELLICOTT'S MILLS STATION,
FIFTEEN MILES FROM BALTIMORE.

Ellicott's Mills (Ellicott City) Station, Baltimore and Ohio Railroad, Maryland.
In the midst of pastoral country, fifteen miles from Baltimore, when this view was published in 1858,
this village on the Patapsco River was the first western terminus of the B. & O.
The station, partially obscured by the end railroad car, was built in 1831.
HAER.

Baltimore and Ohio Railroad Station, Martinsburg, West Virginia.
Many of the first stations originally served other purposes.
That in Martinsburg was built in 1840 as a hotel and was converted for railroad use in 1866.
H. H. Harwood, Jr.

CENTRAL RAILROAD DEPOT, ROCHESTER, N. Y.

New York Central Railroad
Depot, Rochester, New York,
c. 1853-5.

*The shed which offered protection to
passengers and railroad stock was
often directly incorporated with the
head station. That of Rochester was,
like the President Street Station in
Baltimore, built in a classic fashion
with a pilastered façade.*

Library of Congress.

Great Central Railway Depot, Detroit, Michigan, late 1840s.
Railroad station architecture was once an exercise in classical restraint.
This view from an 1850 edition of the Illustrated London News *illustrates the chaste*
conservative taste of early architects and engineers. Even the magnificently domed roundhouse
suggests an appeal to antiquity.
Library of Congress.

President Street Station, Philadelphia, Wilmington and Baltimore Railroad,
Baltimore, Maryland, 1850.
*This simple structure, built to handle passenger and freight traffic, is seen in two views,
the first from 1856 and the second from 1936. As originally conceived, the building
was an impressive temple to classical good taste.*
Sketch, Library of Congress; photograph, Edgar H. Pickering, HABS.

Central of Georgia Passenger Station,
Savannah, Georgia, c. 1855.
Again, the classical façade comes into play.
The design of the Federal-style building would have been hopelessly dated
in a larger metropolitan center in northeastern America or England
where the Italianate or Tuscan style had taken hold,
but it was just right for this area.
The building now serves as a visitors' center.
Louis Schwartz, HABS, 1962.

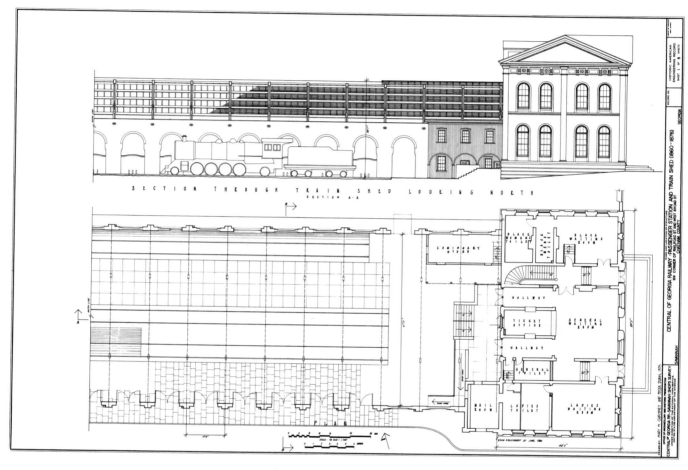

Measured drawing,
Central of Georgia Passenger Station and Train Shed.
The head station form is clearly delineated in this drawing.
Mary M. Chrisney and Peter Dubin, HAER, 1975.

**Camden Street Station,
Baltimore and Ohio Railroad,
1852-6.**
*As originally conceived in 1851,
Baltimore's new city depot was
a somewhat incongruous mixture
of Georgian, Greek Revival, and the
newly popular Italianate styles.
Stripped in time of its adornment
and triumphal towers, its
basic classical inspiration appears predominant.
The building was designed by
Baltimore architect J. F. Kemp.
Drawing, Library of Congress;
photograph, William Edmund Barrett,
HAER, 1970.*

Waiting Room, Camden Street Station.
Passengers in what was once the most monumental of American stations
were provided with a suitably impressive, spacious interior.
Most railroad structures of the time barely provided for the public's comfort.
William Edmund Barrett, HAER, 1970.

Hudson River Railroad
Passenger Station,
New York, New York,
c. 1850.
This view dates from 1869,
a time when West Broadway
and Chambers Street
comprised the heart of
the metropolis. As is visible,
conditions were still primitive
for passengers.
Museum of History and
Technology,
Smithsonian Institution.

Grand Central Depot,
New York & Harlem, New York Central, and New York and New Haven railroads,
New York, New York, 1869-71.
Designed by Isaac C. Buckhout and J. B. Snook for Commodore Vanderbilt's New York Central,
this was the first Grand Central and the last word in railroad elegance.
According to historian Carroll L. V. Meeks,
"It was not until the building of old Grand Central . . . that America had a
single station capable of standing comparison with the finest European ones."
Three stories high and topped with three square-domed pavilions on the 42nd Street side,
the station's design was clearly inspired by the Louvre.
Library of Congress.

**Grand Trunk Railroad Depot,
Durand, Michigan, late nineteenth century.**
*In this view from 1905, American railroading reached at least a new pictorial zenith.
Two lines, the Ann Arbor and Grand Trunk, crossed at this important junction.
Six different trains are seen calling at the late Romanesque Revival station.
Library of Congress.*

If early American railroad company executives were not particularly solicitous of their passengers' comfort, they were concerned about maintaining the proper condition of their rolling stock as well as the freight which paid more and more of the costs of operation. Engineering, of course, was an activity required of even the smallest of lines at the very beginning of their incorporation. Railroading has always been as much the business of engineers, civil and otherwise, as of architects or accountants. Benjamin Henry Latrobe, II, son of the famed architect, served as the first chief engineer of the fledgling Baltimore and Ohio Railroad, and built the important Thomas stone viaduct still standing and in use today (see page 55). The first train sheds erected were little more than wooden barns, and these were soon to be found unsafe and inadequate for the rapidly increasing flow of traffic. The 1869-71 Grand Central Depot in New York was the first to be built with a truly expansive car house or shed of cast iron.

From this time on until the turn of the century, the major railroad companies vied to win the honor of spanning the greatest distance with iron and, later, steel.

Many of these high-vaulted, single-span sheds were only nominally coordinated in design with the head house stations that served as their façades. It is as if the engineers, striving to attain new technological heights, and the architects, merely concerned with the amenities of style, rarely could or were not allowed to work together on a unified concept for the two elements. Still, the great single-span, truss-roofed glass cages were singular accomplishments of lasting significance. Unfortunately, there are only eleven such train sheds left standing in the United States. As Carroll L. V. Meeks has commented, "The railroad companies, finding them very costly to maintain, began to feel toward them as an elderly gentleman feels toward the fading but still extravagant mistress of his youth."

Calvert Station, Baltimore and Susquehanna Railroad,
Baltimore, Maryland, 1848.
J. R. Niernsee and J. C. Nielson designed their Italianate edifice
(see page 45) with an especially generous shed.
This covered five lines and three platforms.
Edgar H. Pickering, HABS, 1936.

Relay House, Baltimore and Ohio Railroad,
Washington Junction (Relay), Maryland, 1850s.
The station provided shelter for rolling stock and passengers in this two-sided arrangement.
It was a through station built in what is also known as the "temple-barn" manner;
that is, an open classical style shed through which trains could pass.
The view dates from 1857.
Museum of History and Technology, Smithsonian Institution.

Atlantic and Great Western Railway Station and McHenry House,
Meadville, Pennsylvania, 1865.
Here again is the open barn form but one worked in a Gothic Revival style.
The complex of buildings, including the spacious McHenry House hotel and restaurant,
was said by the New York Herald in 1870 to "rival in style and beauty of . . . surroundings
any of those you may notice in the best railroads of England;
there are charming cottages for the officers of the road, a park at the rear with winding walks,
fir trees, rose and jessamine bushes."
Museum of History and Technology, Smithsonian Institution.

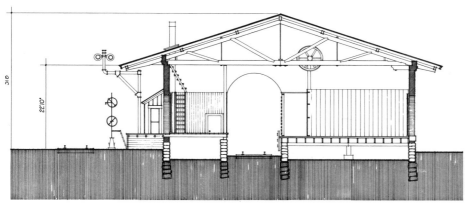

TRANSVERSE SECTION

New Albany and Salem Railroad (Monon)
Passenger and Freight Station, Gosport, Indiana, c. 1854.
This structure is the only known surviving example of the train barn form in the United States.
It was, in part, a through station, with freight trains entering the portico on one side and exiting on the other;
passengers used the outside lines.
Shown here, as well, is a view of the interior freight line and a measured
drawing of the functional wood-trussed structure.
Photographs, Jack E. Boucher,
HAER, 1974; drawing, Mike "Hoosier" Boles, HAER, 1973.

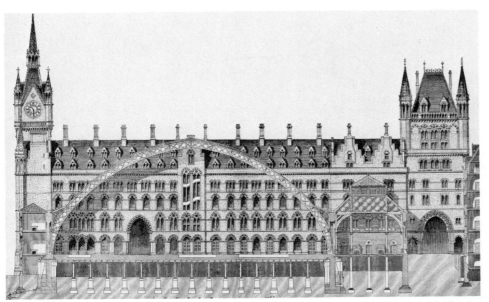

St. Pancras Station,
London, England,
1863-76.
*Sir George Gilbert Scott was
the architect of this building
for the Midland Railway
which so influenced the
design of American stations,
particularly their sheds.
Engineers on the project were
W. H. Barlow and
R. M. Ordish and their work
in the open arched shed
was no less admirable than
the effects of Sir George.
It had a clear span of
243 feet and matched the
station in Gothic elegance.
The exterior view shows
the profile of the shed.
These views are from an
1869 edition of
Building News.*

Car House,
Grand Central Depot,
New York, New York,
1869-71.
*St. Pancras was the model for
the first great American
shed and station, both
designed by Isaac C. Buckhout and J. B. Snook
(see page 36).
It was made of imported
metal that was fabricated by
the famed Architectural Iron
Works of New York.
The shed spanned 200 feet,
reached a height of 100 feet,
and extended behind the
42nd Street station for 600
feet. Museum of History
and Technology,
Smithsonian Institution.*

Reading Terminal, Philadelphia, Pennsylvania, 1891-3.

The Philadelphia and Reading Railroad was embarked on a truly monumental edifice on the site of the center city farmer's market (see page 106)
F. H. Kimball served as architect, and Wilson Brothers and Co. provided additional architectural and engineering expertise. The latter firm also served the Pennsylvania Railroad during its two Broad Street building projects. The Reading single-span shed, one of the last surviving in America today, measures 256 feet wide, short of Broad Street's, but is nonetheless an important engineering feat, HAER, 1976.

 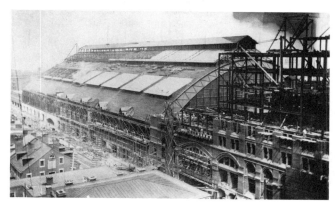

Broad Street Station, Pennsylvania Railroad, Philadelphia, Pennsylvania, 1892-3.

Frank Furness and Allan Evans were the architects employed to redo the 1881 station and to better that then being erected by the Reading. They succeeded admirably in the station itself (see page 73) and in the 300-foot single-span, then the largest in the world. The photograph was taken in 1893 during construction. Pennsylvania Railroad.

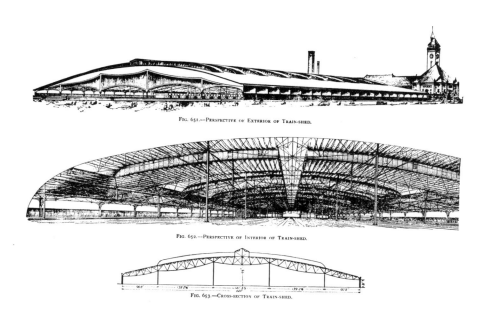

FIG. 651.—PERSPECTIVE OF EXTERIOR OF TRAIN-SHED.

FIG. 652.—PERSPECTIVE OF INTERIOR OF TRAIN-SHED.

FIG. 653.—CROSS-SECTION OF TRAIN-SHED.

Union Station, St. Louis, Missouri, 1891-5.

Theodore C. Link and Edward B. Cameron won the design competition for one of America's most imaginative urban stations (see also page 83.) Simply in terms of size, the train shed engulfed all others standing and most built since that time throughout the world. It measures 600 feet wide, double that of Broad Street, and reaches out 630 feet. The span, however, is not a single one but is, rather, borne on four intermediate supports. Building and Sketches of American Railroads, 1904.

IV
THE RAILROAD STYLE

The first recognizable style to become identified with railroad station architecture was the Italianate. So closely allied did the two become, in fact, that the term "Railroad Style" is now synonymous with the Tuscan or Italian villa form. To some extent Americans were following English fashion; stations of this design were built there during the 1830s. The style became established in the New World's sophisticated urban centers somewhat later, in the late 1840s and early '50s. No doubt A. J. Downing was influential in popularizing this somewhat pretentious if not portentous manner of building. The early railroad companies were now well established and eager to dramatize their economic and social power. What better way than to dress their most publicly accessible buildings in the trappings of picturesque antiquity?

Historian Carroll L. V. Meeks suggests that "the Italian villa style and its cousins offered the opportunity to build cheaply and impressively. . . . A bell, to announce the arrival of trains, and a clock were normal station equipment, and they justified the expense of a campanile. It was not difficult to group picturesquely the necessary buildings and train shed around a tower, provided that orthodox proportions were not demanded." As all the following illustrations show, both sheds and passenger stations proper were gracefully accommodated in the revival style, entryways for both trains and people set forth in the manner of arcaded loggias. The clock tower (or towers) would continue as a staple of railroad-station architecture until at least the end of the century.

Calvert Station, Baltimore and
Susquehanna Railroad,
Baltimore, Maryland, 1848.
Niernsee and Nielson's station (see page 39)
was one of the first in the Italianate style.
Here it seems to have evolved quite naturally
from the Georgian or Federal.
The earlier view, c. 1853,
captures the romantic mood more expressly than the later.
Photograph, Edgar H. Pickering,
HABS, 1936.

Union Railroad Company Depot,
Troy, New York, 1857.
An especially gifted and now unknown architect
supplied not only handsome office space
and waiting rooms
for seven railroads serving
this important transportation center,
but also a functional shed which spanned ten tracks.
Library of Congress.

Western Maryland Railroad Station, Gettysburg, Pennsylvania, 1858.
An almost perfect Italianate villa with a cupola serving as a tower, the Gettysburg building
is that in which Abraham Lincoln arrived in 1863 to deliver his famous address.
A replica of the station which no one could possibly confuse with the original, has been built a mile away.
Photograph, H. H. Harwood, Jr., 1969.

Baltimore and Ohio Railroad Passenger Depot, Wheeling, West Virginia, 1850s.
This photograph dates from 1891.
The B. & O. reached the Ohio River and the city of Wheeling in 1853.
Museum of History and Technology, Smithsonian Institution.

Baltimore and Ohio Railroad Passenger Station, Washington, D. C., 1851.
The B. & O.'s first Washington station was a makeshift affair fashioned from a three-story brick home in 1835. By 1850, an impressive building in the new "Railroad Style" was clearly called for.
Museum of History and Technology, Smithsonian Institution.

Union Station, Charleston, South Carolina, c. 1850-1870.
Variations on the Italian villa style continued in vogue until the late nineteenth century.
An admixture of Italianate, Gothic, and Spanish Colonial elements,
it is a top-heavy mid-Victorian curiosity piece.
The view dates from c. 1895-1900.
Library of Congress.

More familiar to the public today than the Italian villa stations are small railroad buildings in the Gothic Revival style. These rustic structures have survived especially well in relatively isolated rural areas of North America. Never considered terribly important buildings, they are, for the most part, the work of untrained builders in the vernacular tradition of architecture. Some are built in nothing more than what Carroll L. V. Meeks calls the *cottage ornée* style, being simply imitations of designs made popular by A. J. Downing, Calvert Vaux, and other arbiters of mid-nineteenth-century architectural fashion.

While the Italianate style balanced horizontal and vertical lines in nearly equal fashion, the Gothic clearly favored the vertical. Windows and doorways were most often fashioned in a thin, pointed manner. In the most picturesque buildings, barge- or verge-boards, finials, elaborate cornices, and other decorative details in wood and cast iron came into play. Few of the buildings represented any serious exercise in Gothic building style, but they were, nonetheless, often extremely inventive, inviting places. From the earliest board and batten structures to Carpenter's Gothic, Stick Style, and Queen Anne, the decorative impulse was not denied expression. As Victorian Gothic, it became the new railroad style.

Urban examples of the Gothic form are difficult to find today; New York's first Grand Central Terminal (1869-71) fell victim to a Beaux Arts replacement in 1903. In a similar manner, Washington's Baltimore and Potomac Railroad Depot (1873-7) was replaced by Daniel Burnham's classic Union Station in 1903—as if the more monumental the building, the shorter its life was to be. Neither of these stations, of course, compared in their heyday with London's splendid St. Pancras, although attempts were made to better the English example. Paradoxically, American architects of the time seem to have succeeded best in modest, smaller-scale buildings. Such a sophisticated structure is the Point of Rocks, Maryland, station, illustrated in this section, once an important junction stop on the Baltimore and Ohio. It has miraculously escaped destruction.

West Brookfield Station,
West Brookfield, Massachusetts, c. 1839.
*Built by the Western Railroad of Massachusetts
(later the Boston and Albany and the New York Central system),
this early Gothic Revival structure still stands
and is now used as a warehouse.
It is similar to the Bernardston, Massachusetts,
station illustrated on page 13 with
Tudor arches and simple vertical board sheathing.
Photograph, H. H. Harwood, Jr.,
Museum of History and Technology,
Smithsonian Institution.*

Martisco Station, Martisco, New York, 1860.
*This sadly abandoned country depot served the Marcellus and Otisco Lake Railroad,
later part of the Rutland Railway Corporation.
The overhanging eaves, supported by lengthy brackets,
throw the building into a dark gloom.
It is the kind of rough-hewn station that English travelers in the nineteenth-century found appalling.
Gilbert Ask, HABS, 1963.*

Delaware, Lackawanna and Western
Passenger and Freight Station,
Vestal, New York, 1881.
*The Gothic Revival style, as defined in America
by Richard Upjohn and others, survived in the country
well into the late nineteenth century.
True Stick Style detailing is to be found
in this pure and simple structure
which now serves as headquarters
for the local historical society.
Jack E. Boucher, HAER, 1971.*

Baltimore and Ohio Railroad Station, Hanover, Maryland, 1870s.
"Jigsaw gingerbread" might well be the stylistic term applied to this insignificant flagstop.
Some country carpenter must have enjoyed applying his skill to the roof ornaments and vergeboards
of the gable. A. J. Downing might have found these too flimsy in appearance, but they have obviously
survived nearly 100 years in relatively good condition.
Museum of History and Technology, Smithsonian Institution.

Baltimore and Ohio Station,
Frederick Junction,
Maryland, 1870s.
The scalloped overhanging decoration
of the eaves is the only
fanciful feature of this
workmanlike structure
with vertical board siding.
As a junction station serving the
new main line and the old main line
to Point of Rocks,
it was a more serious
place of business than
the usual country depot.
The view probably dates from c. 1900.
Museum of History and Technology,
Smithsonian Institution.

Cedar Hollow Railroad Station, Tredyffrin Township, Pennsylvania, 1872.
First a Chester Valley Railroad and then a Reading station, this building
could have served as a home just as well.
Its design was a standard one for a number of Reading buildings.
which did incorporate living quarters for the stationmaster and his family.
Ned Goode, HABS, 1958.

Reading Railroad Station, Myerstown, Pennsylvania, mid-nineteenth century.
The builders of this Swiss-cottage style station probably never envisioned
advertising posters adorning the exterior, not to speak
of a penny scale and a Bell telephone sign.
The view probably dates from c. 1915.
Library of Congress.

Erie Railroad Depot, Goshen, New York, 1865.
Although stripped to the essentials and worn with time, the waiting room of most country stations was not a thing of great beauty or comfort. The pot-belly stove was a fixture in most of them. Jack E. Boucher, HAER, 1971.

New Jersey and New York Railroad Station,
Woodridge, New Jersey, late nineteenth century.
Typical Gothic forms strongly define this northeast Jersey suburban station.
The New Jersey and New York is now part of the Erie Lackawanna system.
Library of Congress.

Baltimore and Ohio Railroad Station, Point of Rocks, Maryland, 1875.
Designed by architect E. Francis Baldwin, this Victorian Gothic building is a successful blend
of rich materials—brick, granite, and sandstone—that have been applied with
a keen sense of color and texture. It stands on the old main line of the B. & O. (via Frederick Junction)
and the railroad's Baltimore and Washington line.
As the measured drawing indicates, Baldwin's structure was an addition
to an already existing early Gothic Revival building.
Photograph, Jack E. Boucher, HAER, 1961; drawing, Tim Wolosz, HAER, 1971.

Relay Station, Relay, Maryland, 1870s.
On the old main line of the Baltimore and Ohio, this is one of the earliest junction stops on the East Coast.
Travelers heading south for Washington branched out at this point
and crossed the Thomas viaduct seen in the upper left.
Named for the first president of the B. & O., the multi-span masonry bridge over the Patapsco River
(the first such bridge in the United States)
was designed by Benjamin Henry Latrobe, II, son of the U. S. Capitol architect.
Relay was the site of an earlier station and hotel and was prior to that
a changing point for stagecoaches and their teams of horses.
Museum of History and Technology, Smithsonian Institution.

Central Railroad of New Jersey Station, Wilkes-Barre, Pennsylvania, late nineteenth century.
William George Burns was the architect of this late-Victorian depot.
Gothic elements come into play with various other forms typical of the Queen Anne period.
As with the Point of Rocks and Relay stations, details were drawn from various sources.
H. H. Harwood, Jr., 1975.

As the network of rail lines grew during the mid-nineteenth century, it was only logical that the business of accommodating passengers would develop. This was true in cities, especially those situated at important places along the main lines. Harrisburg, Meadville, and Altoona, Pennsylvania —all substantial centers of early rail transportation—once had palatial residential buildings which were linked with stations. Just as airlines today have invested capital in the accommodation of travelers, so, too, did the great railroad companies of the past. New York's Commodore Hotel, now awaiting disposal by the Conrail system, as well as the Biltmore and Roosevelt, are still tied to Grand Central Terminal. The railroads were also in the resort business, the Queen City Hotel, Viaduct Hotel, and Starrucca House being specific examples illustrated in these pages. Great encouragement was given to rail excursions—to the Delaware Water Gap, Yellowstone and Yosemite, Lake Geneva and the Wisconsin Dells, the Adirondacks and the Berkshires.

The most interesting of the buildings were those known as combination stations: that is, depots offering the passenger all services, including room and board, under one roof. By the late nineteenth century most of these multi-purpose stations were to be found only in the West and Southwest, areas where the niceties of civilization might be in short supply. An important publication of the 1890s, *Buildings and Structures of American Railroads* by Walter G. Berg, stated that many a "regularly equipped hotel is connected with the depot, with office, hotel lobby, restaurant and appurtenances, parlors, reading-rooms, writing-room, bedrooms for guests and the hotel help, toilet-rooms, lavatories, billiard-rooms, etc." The Union Pacific's Transfer Depot and Hotel in Council Bluffs, Iowa, was such an institution, and so, too, were U.P. stations of the time in Ogden, Utah, and Cheyenne, Wyoming. Many of the early Atchison, Topeka and Sante Fe stations were also renowned for their hospitable accommodations, if not their fine Fred Harvey restaurants. Dining at the depot was once a treat and not a threat to one's health. Americans, today, must travel in Europe to find a suitable menu.

Queen City Hotel and Station,
Baltimore and Ohio Railroad, Cumberland, Maryland, 1871-2.
*One of the most unfortunate victims of the wrecker's ball (in 1972),
Queen City was designed by architect John W. Garrett.
Located in the mountainous area of western Maryland, the hotel was a convenient and gracious resting place
for summer visitors. It was built in the Italianate style and featured a large octagonal cupola
and decoratively bracketed windows. The dining room stretched the whole length of the center two-story
section. At the time of its destruction, the building was listed on the National Register of Historic Sites.
Museum of History and Technology, Smithsonian Institution.*

Pennsylvania Railroad Station and Logan House,
Altoona, Pennsylvania, mid- and late-nineteenth century.
*The Logan House hotel, as seen in the 1900 drawing and 1890s photograph, is nearly identical with Queen
City. It, too, featured a center section crowned with a cupola and framed by two massive side wings.
The freestanding cast-iron shed is a particularly handsome structure.
The Romanesque building to the left in the photograph, built at a later date,
was demolished along with the hotel in 1930.
Museum of History and Technology, Smithsonian Institution.*

Relay Station and Viaduct Hotel,
Relay, Maryland, 1870s.
*This view from 1881 shows the station/hotel
at the height of its splendor—
as both a changing point for the
Baltimore and Ohio's Washington and main lines,
and as a country resting spot.
HAER.*

Susquehanna Station and Starrucca House,
Susquehanna, Pennsylvania, 1865.
*Susquehanna was an important stop on the Erie Railroad's main line west between New York and
Dunkirk, New York; a branch line left here for Scranton and Wilkes-Barre and provided a link
with the coal area. Attributed to architect E. J. M. Derrick, it still stands today and alternative uses for it
are being sought. By 1903 restaurant and hotel service ceased and the building
was converted for railroad offices and a railroad YMCA.
Photograph, Jack E. Boucher, HAER, 1971.*

NORTH (TRACKSIDE) ELEVATION

SCALE: 1" = 20'

Susquehanna Station and Starrucca House, Susquehanna, Pennsylvania, 1865.
These drawings show the north elevation, the front doors, and the sketch of the cupola.
North elevation, Charles Parrott, HAER; front doors, George Yee, HAER; cupola, Smithsonian Institution.

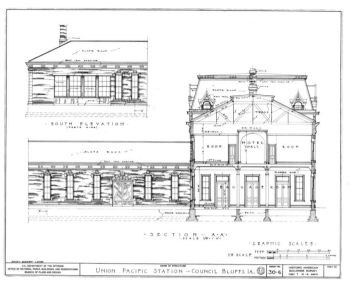

Union Pacific Transfer Depot and Hotel,
Council Bluffs, Iowa, 1887.
*Some sense of the arrangement of space
in a combination terminal and hotel
is given in this side view of
what was the U.P.'s eastern terminal.
The building was located some distance
from the depots for the Chicago and Great Western;
Chicago and North Western; Chicago, Milwaukee,
St. Paul, and Pacific; Chicago, Rock Island, and Pacific;
and Burlington, in what
was its own separate town—Council Bluffs Transfer.
HABS.*

Fred Harvey Lunch Room,
Santa Fe Railroad Station (Union Station), San Diego, California, 1914-15.
*A noonday meal was a pleasure in the immaculate and inviting Fred Harvey restaurant,
one of a chain stretching west from Chicago.
Whether cut flowers were always provided is questionable,
but there is no doubt that food was attractively served and prepared.
The photo dates from c. 1915.
Library of Congress.*

Henry Hobson Richardson (1838-1886) was the first American architect to radically change the form of railroad station design. Although not as active an architect of buildings for railroad companies as was a contemporary, Frank Furness, Richardson broke firmly with Victorian Gothic practice. His stations, all of them constructed in the 1880s, alone constituted a new definition of the "railroad style." Romanesque Revival is a term that is now considered to be nearly synonymous with the new Richardsonian style as articulated not only by the master himself but by his many disciples.

The stations built for the Boston and Albany Railroad in the Boston area are the most noteworthy. Henry-Russell Hitchcock has described the first of these in Auburndale as "no more than a long low rectangle of rock-faced granite covered with a roof." And that it is. It is only in the massing of shapes, especially that of the low roof with overhanging eaves which enfold the heavy masonry walls, that something original has been created. The buildings are deeply rooted, horizontally contoured structures making use of earthy, natural materials. Critic Vincent Scully calls them "archetypes of movement and stability synthesized. . . . They were both urban and suburban place-fixing masses adjusted to explanding suburban patterns along the commuting railroad lines."

Richardson's buildings will be analyzed forever for they have the imaginative quality which transcends the ornamental. His unique contribution, however, perhaps may be best seen in the most simple of artifacts marking a milestone in North American railroad history—the Sherman, Wyoming, monument commemorating the construction of the Union Pacific. It is nothing but a massive ashlar pyramid in which are set two bronze plaques by Augustus Saint-Gaudens to Oakes and Oliver Ames of North Easton and Boston, Massachusetts, financiers and builders of the railroad. Frederick L. Ames, the son of Oliver, was Richardson's great patron. The architect surely could have fashioned a monument which reflected his own aesthetic training at the Ecole des Beaux Arts, Paris, but, rather, he turned to a striking sculptural form which is every bit as natural and dramatic as the rugged landscape in which it is set. Richardson's remaining stations are similar monuments to genius.

Boston and Albany Railroad Station,
Wellesley, Massachusetts, 1884.
*The trackside exterior and waiting room of this Richardson station,
sadly demolished now, graphically illustrate his bold and imaginative use
of natural building materials.
The interior, in particular, expresses within fairly limited space
the way in which structural elements can provide an appealing mood,
a play of light, a feeling of texture.
Cervin Robinson, HABS, 1959.*

Old Colony Railroad Station, North Easton, Massachusetts, 1886.
*Among the five Richardson buildings commissioned by patron F. L. Ames in North Easton
was this fortress-like edifice. The quarry-faced stone, stone voussoirs or arches,
and widely overhanging roof combine to create an air of absolute achitectural invincibility.
The building has been preserved by the local historical society.
Cervin Robinson, HABS, 1959.*

Boston and Albany Railroad Station,
Framingham, Massachusetts, 1883.
Again, Richardson used strong building materials with dramatic effect—
the quarry-faced stone walls, the bow-front stationmaster's window set with bulls-eye glass panes,
the waiting room's open ceiling truss of structural iron beams
criss-crossing in seeming defiance of gravity.
Cervin Robinson, HABS, 1959.

Boston and Albany Railroad Station,
Auburndale, Massachusetts, 1881.

The first Richardson B. & A. station uses rough, random ashlar of red and light-gray granite,
brownstone trimmings, and once was roofed in red tiles.
These have been replaced with asbestos shingles.
Seen to the side is the porte cochere *which,*
defying common architectural practice of the time, has been totally integrated
with the building and its roof line.
Cervin Robinson, HABS, 1959.

Boston and Albany Railroad Station, Palmer, Massachusetts, 1881.
*The main lines of the B. & A. and the Central Vermont Railroad
(formerly New London and Norwich Railroad) cross at this point.
Richardson designed a station in the shape of a trapezoid to fit the space formed by the two lines.
The familiar Richardsonian curved spaces are graphically evident.
Cervin Robinson, HABS, 1959.*

Union Railroad Station, New London, Connecticut, 1885-87.
*The two-and-a-half story red brick building serving the New York, New Haven and Hartford,
and Central Vermont railroads was commissioned in September, 1885,
only a short time before Richardson's death the following Spring.
His chronicler, Henry-Russell Hitchcock, claims the station to have been formed
under the architect's early direction.
The imaginative brick detailing in the cornice and gable
and the use of well-integrated dormer windows certainly mark the building
as one of Richardson's most successful.
Long the scene of a community preservation battle,
the building has finally been saved for the future.
Jack E. Boucher, HABS, 1973*

VIII

THE ECLECTICISM OF FRANK FURNESS

Frank Furness (1839-1912) was among the most prolific and idiosyncratic of designers of American railroad stations. A member of a brilliant Philadelphia family, he apprenticed under Richard Morris Hunt in New York and returned in 1866 to begin a career that would center almost exclusively in the Philadelphia area. His masterpieces are Victorian Gothic structures of a rather top-heavy sort in which a wide variety of *neo-grec,* Romanesque, Moorish, and Gothic forms are given imaginative play. Added to these design elements which, in theory seem so disparate, is ornamentation of a highly colorful, naturalistic type.

Furness's most successful station, the Chestnut Street building for the Baltimore and Ohio, is not as imaginative as his early work such as the Pennsylvania Academy of Fine Arts (1871-76) or the Guarantee Trust Company building (1875), but it is nonetheless a unique structure, as were almost all those designed by the architect. Commissions from the Philadelphia and Reading, Pennsylvania, and Baltimore and Ohio railroads came in mid-career to Furness and his firm of the late nineteenth century, Furness, Evans and Company. Unfortunately, most of the large stations have been destroyed, including Furness's last great edifice, the enlargement of the Broad Street Station. There are, however, some suburban depots remaining, most of them built during the time he designed almost exclusively for the Reading. Notable among these is the Graver's Lane building.

Furness's designs were highly praised and prized in his own day. "The entire design is finished off very artistically, and presents a very handsome appearance," wrote one commentator of the Tabor, Pennsylvania, depot for the Reading. This architect's reputation, however, went into a sharp decline by the turn of the century and has been resurrected only recently.

Baltimore and Ohio Station (Chestnut Street),
Philadelphia, Pennsylvania, 1886-1888.
Of the many stations designed by Furness, Chestnut Street was most deserving of preservation,
but it was destroyed in the early 1960s. As these three exterior views show, the multi-faceted structure
was richly ornamented in detail and conceived with a masterful grasp of mass effects.
The clock tower is probably the most distinctive Furness touch,
its Gothic lines being repeated again and again in gables, dormers, and the porte cochere.
The photograph dates from the 1920s, the drawing is c. 1890.
Photograph, Museum of History and Technology, Smithsonian Institution;
measured drawing, Craig Morrison, HABS, 1968;
drawing, F. E. Lummis, Smithsonian Institution.

Interior views, Baltimore and Ohio Station.
*Furness's love and mastery of decorative detailing is encountered almost everywhere
in the massive inner spaces of the Chestnut Street station.
The ornamentation is found in the waiting room's grand staircase with elaborately-worked iron railings
and lighting fixtures, above a pair of arched fireplaces, and in the carved wood benches of the waiting room.
Photographs, Cervin Robinson, HABS, 1959.*

Baltimore and Ohio Station, Chester, Pennsylvania, 1886.
*Furness, Evans and Company's Chester building was considered less flamboyant in form
than that of Philadelphia's Chestnut Street Station;
it partakes of more of the then popular Shingle Style.
The interplay of different roof lines, the clock tower, and the dormers
combine to form a distinctive Furness profile.
Museum of History and Technology, Smithsonian Institution.*

Baltimore and Ohio Passenger Station, Pittsburgh, Pennsylvania, 1888.
*A massive block centered on a clock tower, this Furness, Evans and Company structure
defies any rational description. It is a brooding structure of a Romanesque massiveness
which partakes of Second Empire and Queen Anne forms.
Granite, brick, shingles, cut-away porches with graceful ironwork, decorative chimneys and brownstone
trimmings all add up to an extremely individualistic if not eccentric composition.
Museum of History and Technology, Smithsonian Institution.*

Broad Street Station, Pennsylvania Railroad,
Philadelphia, Pennsylvania, 1892-3.
*Frank Furness and partner Allan Evans were the architects chosen
to substantially alter and enlarge a station built in 1881.
Added to a simple six-story Gothic design station built in 1881-2 (seen at right)
was an eleven-story building crowned with
an extraordinary medieval tower worthy of the sketchbooks of Viollet-le Duc.
The interior appointments were similarly fanciful and accomplished.
The architect's rendering dates from 1893.
Courtesy, Pennsylvania Railroad.*

IX

THE NEW RAILROAD STYLE

As the reputation and influence of Furness began to decline in the 1880s, that of Richardson was only beginning to rise. The most notable architect who is known to have worked with Furness, Louis Sullivan, while owing some aspects of his work to the Philadelphia master, was to build on the Romanesque Revival tradition for his aesthetic. Richardson's followers, many of them employed at one time in his Brookline, Massachusetts, office, were to define further the canon of Romanesque style after his death in 1888. John Shepley, Charles Rutan, and Charles A. Coolidge continued the Richardson firm under their own names; Charles McKim and Stanford White were to go on to fashion the rustic Shingle Style, which, in the interweaving of gable and gambrel roof, partakes of the coming Colonial Revival and the past massive Richardsonian masonry profile.

In the South and Midwest Richardson's award-winning public buildings were regarded with considerable respect. New stations were required in almost every major city, and it is not surprising to see, in retrospect, that the railroad companies should have turned to the Richardsonian Romanesque for their basic model. These stations, however, were not suburban depots, but urban terminals requiring a multiplicity of facilities. Most were "union" stations; that is, terminals serving several different railroads and managed and/or owned by the leading line or a terminal association.

Although designed by different architects, the union stations of Nashville, Louisville, and Indianapolis bear a striking resemblance to each other. None of the three is completely divorced in style from the High Victorian Gothic aesthetic of previous decades. The small stations illustrated here from various parts of the country, with the exception of that in Dubuque, Iowa, more closely approximate the Richardsonian Romanesque. Both the St. Louis and the Duluth stations express another aspect of 1890s eclecticism, the French Romanesque or Norman style. All these buildings, however, make use of the basic Romanesque Revival vocabulary of rough-hewn stone massed in a monumental manner and of the slender clock tower or campanile, the sole vertical element to rise from the heavily horizontal contour.

Chicago's Grand Central Station stands (or did stand, having been foolishly demolished in the 1960s) as a singular example of the pure Romanesque Revival form adapted to urban use. A brilliantly conceived and executed building by Spencer Solon Beman, its simple lines dramatically foreshadows the further streamlining which was soon to come at the hands of Sullivan and Wright.

Erie Railroad Station, Middletown, New York, c. 1880-1.
The arched entryway to the Middletown station simply expresses the nature of the Romanesque Revival,
the centrality of heavy masonry construction in a vaulted manner.
Middletown was an important point on the main line where the Erie met the once-thriving New York,
Ontario and Western Railroad, and a minor branch line, the Middletown
and Unionville Railway (Middletown and New Jersey).
Both the exterior and interior appointments emphasize the special attention
given to this early Erie terminus.
Jack E. Boucher, HAER, 1971.

Union Station, Nashville, Tennessee, 1900.
*Richard Montfort was the designer of this monumental station serving
the Louisville and Nashville, and Tennessee Central railroads.
Montfort, chief engineer of the L. & N. was obviously influenced by Richardson's work,
especially his Allegheny County Court House and Jail in Pittsburgh.
Jack E. Boucher, HABS, 1970.*

Interior, Union Station.
The general waiting room was praised in its heyday as especially spacious and tasteful.
It stands empty now, the roof having been declared unsound.
The city of Nashville is exploring alternative uses.
Jack E. Boucher, HABS, 1970.

Exterior ornamentation,
Union Station.
*Bowling Green gray stone
and Tennessee marble was used
in the construction
of the building. The extremely
rich and fine carving
of the stone and the use of
ornamental cast-iron railings
further embellish an
already distinguished
public building.
Jack E. Boucher, HABS, 1970.*

Union Station, Louisville, Kentucky, 1882-91.
*The Louisville and Nashville's main terminal, built of pressed bricks and ornamental limestone,
was designed by architect H. Wolters.
It served two other rail lines,
the Pennsylvania and the Chicago, Indianapolis and Louisville (Monon).
Dan Finfrock, Collection of H. H. Harwood, Jr.*

Union Station, Indianapolis, Indiana, 1886-9.
Architect Thomas Rodd designed a most impressive urban edifice for a growing metropolis.
The basic stone and brick turreted and towered structure is
ornamented and defined in almost every respect.
The dramatic wheel or rose window of medieval inspiration shines forth
as a symbol of the wealth and imagination
of the high Victorian railroad age in which
the dynamo was fast replacing the Virgin as a tenet of faith.
Jack E. Boucher, HABS, 1970.

Grand Central Station,
Chicago, Illinois, 1888-90.
*Now gone is one of Chicago's
great architectural treasures
designed by Spencer Solon Beman.
The Romanesque has been stripped clean
of Gothic fancywork, and
the tower raised to a new height—
in this case, 247 feet.
The building is solidly anchored
by massive arched and sloping
stone piers which predate those
of Burnham and Root's
Monadnock Building.
Museum of History and Technology,
Smithsonian Institution.*

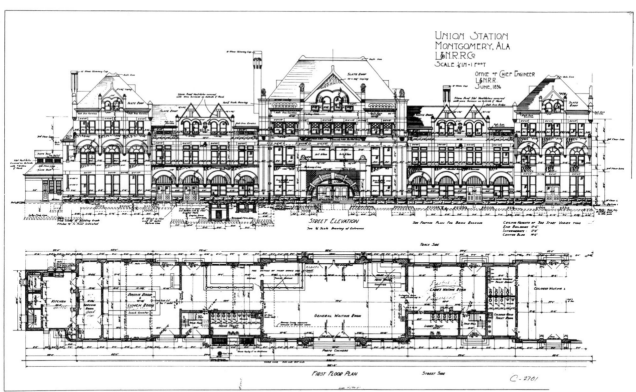

Union Railroad Station, Montgomery, Alabama, 1897-8.
*Benjamin Bosworth Smith was the architect of Montgomery's combined station serving several lines,
most notably the Louisville and Nashville.
The original drawing shows in detail the massing of Victorian Gothic and Romanesque
Revival forms typical of the period. The first floor plan gives
a good idea of the layout of waiting rooms in such a station south of the Mason-Dixon line—
"general" for gentlemen; a separate ladies' reception area;
and completely isolated facilities for "colored" persons.
HAER.*

Illinois Central Railroad Station,
Dubuque, Iowa, 1887.
This small city on the Mississippi
was once the meeting ground
for four rail lines:
the IC, the Burlington, the Chicago and Great Western,
and the Chicago, Milwaukee, St. Paul and Pacific.
Each had a separate station. •
Typically high Victorian in style,
the Dubuque building illustrated here
rather incongruously mixes
Gothic Revival and Romanesque Revival forms
in the gables and tower.
Library of Congress.

Delaware, Lackawanna and Western
Railroad Station, Binghamton, New York,
c. 1885-1890.
The Italianate railroad style of
the mid-century still lingers
in the tower of this upstate
New York station.
The sloping hip roof,
however, is reminiscent of the lower,
more horizontal lines of
the Richardsonian Romanesque.
Jack E. Boucher, HABS, 1966.

Michigan Central Railroad Depot,
Battle Creek, Michigan, 1887-88.
Again is seen the combination
of clock tower (72 feet high)
and sloping hip roof sweeping
into broad eaves.
The porte cochere is not merely attached,
but is formed naturally by
the gabled section at left.
The building was designed
by the Detroit firm
of Rogers and McFarlane.
Allen Stross, HABS, 1965.

New Haven Railroad Station,
Stoughton, Massachusetts, 1887-8.
Attributed to the Boston firm of Sturgis and Brigham,
this handsome structure was built of local granite
by the Boston and Providence Railroad,
later merged with the New York,
New Haven, and Hartford.
The masonry work is especially fine,
especially as seen in the tower with
its medieval "loophole" windows.

Union Station, St. Louis, Missouri, 1891-5.
*Theodore C. Link and Edward B. Cameron won a major design competition for this most splendid
of Romanesque-style urban railroad buildings.
It was constructed of Missouri grey granite. The tower rises 200 feet. The shed (see also page 43)
extends 600 feet behind the station and is more than 600 feet wide.
Here the Romanesque has been treated in the French style that has become known as Norman Revival.
The view dates from 1894.
Library of Congress.*

Union Depot, Duluth, Minnesota, 1892.
*Duluth turned to the then popular Norman Revival style as interpreted by
the architectural firm of Peabody, Sterns, and Furber.
The similarity between the center section of the St. Louis terminal and this Northern city is striking.
The building is one that has been successfully "recycled" for use as a cultural center.
Lyman E. Nylander.*

X
THE SPANISH INFLUENCE

As the procession of architectural revivals of past styles continued apace throughout the nineteenth century, it was only natural that the Spanish Colonial or Mission Revival style should emerge. Large portions of the United States, of course, were settled by persons owing more of their cultural heritage to Spain than to northern European countries. And it is no wonder that, in the general revival of Colonial fashion in building underway during the 1880s and '90s, the adobe missions of the Southwest and West should be held up as models for such important public structures as railroad stations. They certainly were as appropriate in form as the rustic Stick Style "Craftsman Homes" being popularized by Gustav Stickley at the same time in the West. The cool, simple Mission stations were almost the antithesis of these highly-ornamented bungalows. In the hands of truly creative architects, the Spanish Colonial was given a form that was both traditionally correct and modern in expression.

Bertram Goodhue, architect of San Diego's 1915 California-Pacific Exposition, is given credit for popularizing the Mission form as an appropriate one for public buildings. The station built in that city in 1914-15, although not designed by Goodhue, is clearly influenced by him. The best example of the style, the Union Pacific Mainline Depot in Boise, Idaho, was built ten years later. The roots of the revival, however, were established much earlier, as witness the Burlingame and Riverside, California, stations illustrated here.

The Spanish influence was also articulated in places and ways far distant from the missions established by the Franciscan fathers. Many of the major cities in the southeastern United States still contain railroad stations built in what can only be called the Spanish Baroque style. Almost all were erected at the turn of the century and follow a more classical Spanish form than the mission. These are palaces worthy of secular princes and not those of the Church.

In yet another area of the country, in the states of Missouri, Oklahoma, and Texas, Spanish-style stations rose during the late nineteenth century. These were located along the lines of the Frisco, Katy, Southern Pacific, and Sante Fe. They were closer in form to the Mission ideal, but were more rough-hewn and haphazard in design. The Sante Fe depot in San Angelo, Texas, illustrated here, is of this sort.

Railroad Terminal Building, San Juan, Puerto Rico, 1913.
Few Spanish Colonial buildings in the mainland United States can compare with even the now fragmentary remains of the San Juan terminal. Masonry walls are covered with stucco; the handsome clock tower is topped with an equilateral dome of concrete construction. Unfortunately the building was not included in the Old San Juan historic district.
Jack E. Boucher, HABS, 1967.

Union Depot, Savannah, Georgia, late nineteenth century.
Mediterranean style might be an apt term to apply to this urban station. In design it owed little to the missions or other early buildings of New Spain. The twin towers, like that of San Juan, are topped with equilateral domes and flag finials. The overall decoration is baroque in composition, and is somewhat incongruous in its application.
Library of Congress.

Terminal Station, Atlanta, Georgia, 1905.
Philip Thornton Marye was the architect of this station serving three lines—the Southern, Atlanta and West Point, and Seaboard. It is a true palace with a recognizably Spanish influence evident in the red tile roofs and ornate porticoes.
The view dates from c. 1910. Library of Congress.

Gulf, Mobile, and Ohio Railroad Station, Mobile, Alabama, 1907.
*Philip Thornton Marye was also the architect of this coastal main station.
It is a freehand expression of the Spanish Baroque style with emphasis given to the principal entryway,
a series of arches forming a graceful portico.
Roy Thigpen, HABS, 1966.*

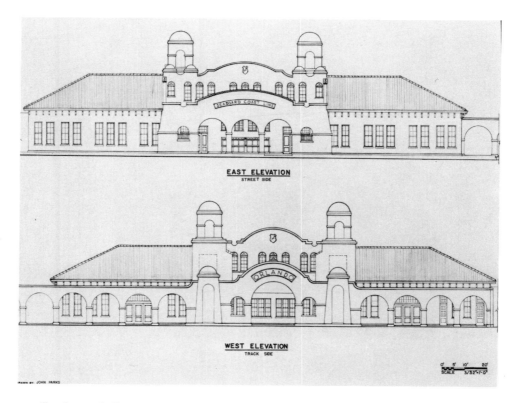

Seaboard Coast Line Railroad Station, Orlando, Florida, 1926.
*Like Mobile, the Orlando station is so composed as to center the viewer's eye
on the massive entryway. On the track side a colonnade stretches the full length of the building
and serves both an aesthetic and practical purpose.
John Parks, HABS.*

Seaboard Air Line Railroad Passenger Station,
West Palm Beach, Florida, 1924-25.
*The Spanish Baroque style was here best expressed and
has been since almost impeccably maintained.
L. Philips Clarke was the architect for the railroad,
many of whose stockholders wintered
in the wealthy resort area.
The elaborate ornament around
windows and portals is especially
well cast and carved.
The track-side façade is
more functional in form than
the general exterior and
offers the passenger
ample protection from the elements.
Jack E. Boucher, HABS, 1972.*

Waiting Room, Seaboard Air Line Passenger Station.
*The fireplace could have warmed at least
the heart of any East-Coast millionaire seeking solace from
a grey Northern winter.
Such fireplaces were de rigueur features
of many urban railroad station
waiting rooms, but not even those of Frank Furness's
Chestnut Street Station could match that
of West Palm Beach.
Jack E. Boucher, HABS, 1972.*

Santa Fe Railroad Depot,
San Angelo, Texas, late nineteenth century.
Typical of many stations in the border South and Texas is that of San Angelo.
The old railroad Italianate style has been translated in the Spanish fashion with
red-tiled roofs and baroque façades.
The view dates from 1908.
Library of Congress.

Southern Pacific Railroad Station,
Riverside, California, late nineteenth century.
The basic underlying hip-roofed form of this Southern California station is Romanesque,
but virtually piggybacked on top of it is a Spanish-design second floor.
The view dates from 1904.
Library of Congress.

Southern Pacific Railroad Station, Burlingame, California, 1894.
Architect George H. Howard is credited with one of the earliest
Mission Style stations in the country.
A view of its handsome garden is sufficient evidence of the special care
which attended the creation of this peaceful, almost spiritual setting.
Baroque decoration has been virtually stripped away and replaced by simple white Colonial walls
broken only by softly arched portals and, at left, quatrefoil windows.
Morley Baer, HABS, 1971.

Union Station,
San Diego, California, 1914-15.
Built for the Atchison, Topeka and Santa Fe, and designed by the firm of Bakewell and Brown,
this building first served visitors attending the California-Pacific Exposition.
The event celebrated the opening of the Panama Canal.
As the site of the oldest Spanish settlement in California,
San Diego was the appropriate setting for a full-blown Mission Style railroad passenger station.
Both the exterior and the colonnade leading to the interior waiting room display a chaste,
cool aesthetic more in keeping with the age of faith than that of capitalism.
Marvin Rand, HABS, 1971.

Union Pacific Mainline Depot,
Boise, Idaho, 1924-5.

Spanish Mission or Colonial style at its most sublime was realized in this building,
designed by the firm of Carrère, Hastings, Shreve and Lamb. Nearly every detail of the cathedral-sized
building is finely realized in these views of the track side and west end. The campanile provides
just the right relief and accompaniment to the long horizontal lines of the station proper.
The U. P. no longer provides passenger service to or out of Boise,
but the company has taken pride in maintaining the building in good condition.
Duane Garrett, HABS, 1974.

Interior, Union Pacific Mainline Depot.
*No one could be faulted for mistaking the inside of this station for that of a church.
The benches might very well be pews.
Colorful floor tiles and fine decorated truss beams provide some relief
to the overwhelming expanse of pure light.
Duane Garrett, HABS, 1974.*

Southern Pacific Railroad Station,
Palm Springs, California,
early 20th century.
This posh Southern California resort community,
equally as fashionable as
the Palm Beach, Florida, area, also boasted
an elegant passenger station.
Its bell tower or campanile
is topped with a most unusual steeple,
sporting a Moorish or Venetian design.
The view dates from c. 1930.

Southern Pacific Depot,
San Francisco, California, 1915.
Built for visitors coming to town for the Panama-Pacific Exposition of 1915,
a competitive attraction to San Diego's affair,
this was an impressive example of Mission Style architecture.
Gradually it was allowed to deteriorate, and, finally, in 1976,
the last portions of it were pulled to the ground.
The view dates from 1971.
Henry E. Bender, Jr., H. H. Harwood, Jr., Collection.

During the late nineteenth century, increasing numbers of stations were built in what can only be called the spirit of Creative Eclecticism. Although many of them are now judged not to be in any sense original in style, it was clear that the architects themselves were attempting a creative synthesis of past forms with the new. Richardson and Furness were among the most successful of these designers. Henry Van Brunt, architect of the Worcester, Massachusetts, station (illustrated in the Introduction) was another accomplished synthesizer. And so, too, were Daniel Burnham and other architects of the Beaux Arts school.

More difficult to analyze and to evaluate are those stations which combine an almost bewildering array of building styles—Gothic, Romanesque, Italianate, Queen Anne, Second Empire. In the United States such children of unknown parentage have not been judged too harshly. A critic of the 1890s, Louis H. Gibson, noted in a book entitled *Beautiful Houses* that, while buildings first must measure up as structurally sound, they can be decorated "with the best motives which the world's architecture has to offer us. If we can do this in an original spirit, it is well, but originality is not essential."

Basic principles for judging such structures are still, nevertheless, necessary. Carroll L. V. Meeks in his definitive history, *The Railroad Station,* combined and rephrased a set of rules or standards which were posited by such nineteenth-century writers as Viollet-le-Duc, Sir George Gilbert Scott, Gottfried Semper, and Henry Van Brunt:

A creative eclectic building should be judged, first, by whether it adheres to the constructive principle involved; second, by whether the exterior is an expression of the interior in either an ideal or a literal sense; third, by whether the forms have been employed with freedom and independence rather than with literal exactness; fourth, by whether the reminiscences have been wisely coordinated and placed in perfect agreement with each other; fifth, by whether it serves the conditions and uses the materials dictated by the age; sixth, by whether the result is simple and comprehensible.

Most of the stations included in this section fail on at least two or three grounds. This, however, does not make them any less interesting or valuable artifacts of a particular time and place. Buildings, as we are constantly reminded today, exist as part of a larger social and economic framework, and even the poorest among them from the past may serve a useful function in defining where we are today, our sense of place.

If there is any common stylistic denominator among these disparate stations, it is to be found in the increasing emphasis given to horizontal dimensions rather than the vertical. While the typical American city or town was stretching upward, the station was being flattened down along the rail lines. Most of the buildings were still monumental and would assume even more ponderous forms in the Beaux Arts period of the early twentieth century, but the railroad station was not much longer to dominate the skyline.

Main Street Station (New Union Station),
Richmond, Virginia, 1901.
*The firm of Wilson, Harris and Richards of Philadelphia was responsible for this
French Renaissance-style building. The long sloping roof
of reddish ceramic tiles rises from an intricately carved parapet.
The passenger platforms are elevated to the left.
The station was built by and served primarily the Chesapeake and Ohio.
Edward F. Heite, HABS, 1969.*

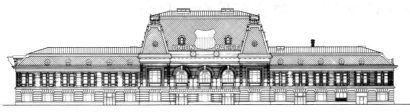

Union Pacific Passenger Depot,
Salt Lake City, Utah, 1909.
*Yet another mansard-roofed structure, this is the design of a U.P. engineer, D. J. Patterson.
A rear view taken in 1924 and a drawing of the east façade display two stylistic tendencies at work—
a Second Empire rendering of the upper roof portion and a more classical, restrained lower half
reminiscent of Beaux Arts design. The building now serves as offices and a communication center for the U.P.
Photograph, Utah State Historical Society;
drawing, Eric V. Ramsing, HABS, 1974.*

Waiting Room,
Union Pacific Passenger Depot.
*The main waiting room is pure Second Empire
in form and, as such, seems more fitting for
the Old World than this pioneer Far Western city.
The charming clerestory windows,
with stained glass scenes
above the ornate cornice, and
the realistic mural at the far end,
also seen in a detail photograph,
bring one home to the West
and its unique railroad history.
Earl Lyman, Utah State Historical Society.*

Central Railroad of New Jersey Station, Bethlehem, Pennsylvania, 1873.
*Bethlehem's high Victorian station has been carefully restored even though it has long since ceased to serve
passengers. In general the building is Second Empire in style with mansard roof and dormer windows,
but the heavily bracketed overhanging roof is cut away in the center to reveal
picturesque Queen Anne form and woodwork.
Jack E. Boucher, HABS, 1969.*

Strafford Station,
Tredyffrin Township, Pennsylvania, 1876.
This is a totally unique station built in Japan
for use as that country's contribution
to the Centennial Exposition.
It was moved from Philadelphia's Fairmount Park
and first served as a station at Wayne.
It has stood at Strafford on the
Pennsylvania Railroad's main line since 1887.
In many ways the building relates
to Stick Style structures found along
the nearby Reading lines,
including some of Frank Furness's stations.
Ned Goode, HABS, 1958.

Cornwall and Lebanon Railroad Station, Lebanon, Pennsylvania, 1885-6.
The original building, designed by George W. Hewitt, was only the part seen to the right;
a difference in the shade of the brick distinguishes the older section from the newer.
In style the building is truly eclectic and incorporates Romanesque, Gothic, Second Empire,
and what might be termed Dutch Colonial elements.
Some of the Delaware and Hudson Railroad stations
of New York state resemble it.
H. H. Harwood, Jr.

**Baltimore and Potomac Railroad Depot,
Washington, D. C., 1873-7.**
*This station served as the terminal for the Washington branch of the Pennsylvania Railroad
and was designed by Joseph M. Wilson, also the architect of that line's first Broad Street Station
in Philadelphia (1881-2). It is the essence of Victorian Gothic,
a confectioner's dream in brick and stone. Like some of the Furness stations, however,
it anticipates a massing of form typical of the post-Victorian period.
The station stood on the ground of the present Union Station.
The photograph was taken in 1881.
Library of Congress.*

Southern Station, Greenville, South Carolina, c. 1890.
Another strange form to the modern eye is here encountered. Remove the tower with its Gothic and
classical touches, and you are left with a Romanesque Revival body.
The view dates from early in this century.
Library of Congress.

Pennsylvania Railroad Station, Lambertville, New Jersey, late nineteenth century.
Located on the Pennsylvania's Belvidere-Delaware Division, this stop was an important one
for travelers from Trenton to such places as New Hope, Pennsylvania, across the Delaware,
and Phillipsburg and Belvidere, New Jersey, to the north.
The stone construction is typical of that used in many stations throughout the valley by this and other
railroads. The roof line is its most distinctive feature, a sort of
abbreviated hip roof in the Queen Anne style known as "jerkinhead."
Robert M. Vogel.

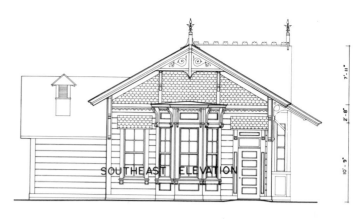

SOUTHEAST ELEVATION

Delaware, Lackawanna and Western
Railroad Station,
Glen Ridge, New Jersey, 1887.
*This suburban station might be
best termed a Shingle Style lodge.
Rustic in appearance, it was so positioned
by architect Jesse H. Lockwood
to take full advantage of
a sandstone cut through which the tracks passed.
It was a handsome building for
affluent suburban commuters
to Newark and New York.
A horse and buggy
is seen entering a porte cochere at far left.
New York Public Library.*

Southern Pacific (San Francisco and San Jose)
Railroad Station,
Menlo Park, California, 1867.
*This is the oldest railroad building
in California still in use.
It is constructed of California redwood
and has been enlarged three times,
last in the 1880s and '90s
with Stick Style ornamentation.
The building is now being used by
the local chamber of commerce.
Amy Weinstein, HABS, 1974.*

Union Pacific Railroad Depot
(Echo and Park City Railroad),
Park City, Utah, c. 1886.
*The town's best-dressed citizens seem
to have gathered for this photograph,
taken in the 1890s.
The station is a picturesque cottage.
The second-story Queen Anne gable porch
must have been a delight for
train buffs of the period.
The design of the building was executed
by U. P. engineers.
Library of Congress.*

Erie Railroad Station,
Tuxedo Park, New York,
and the
Kensington Avenue Passenger Depot,
Buffalo, New York,
both dating from the 1880s.
*Tuxedo Park's station,
with motorcar entering the porte cochere,
may have been built first as
a model suburban railroad building
by the line's engineering department.
The community was the
private preserve of
extremely wealthy New Yorkers,
some of whom probably
owned shares in the Erie.
In this photo, dating from around 1912,
the structure has been well maintained.
The Buffalo station was already
going to pieces in 1913
when the second photograph was taken.
Tuxedo Park: Library of Congress;
Kensington Avenue, HAER.*

Missouri Pacific Railroad Station,
Kirkwood, Missouri,
early twentieth century.
The Mo Pac suburban station
west of St. Louis is typical
in many respects of those
built throughout the Midwest
by other railroads,
including the Chicago and North Western,
the Milwaukee Road, and the Rock Island,
particularly for use by commuters.
Massive, Shingle Style structures
of brick or stone,
they hugged the ground in
Richardsonian manner.
Unlike the stations
more directly derived from
the Romanesque Revival,
however, these were somewhat
boxy, gloomy buildings.
Paul Piaget, HABS, 1967.

Union Pacific Passenger Depot
(Oregon Short Line),
Logan, Utah, c. 1898.
Stations in many parts of the West
were not built in the
Spanish Colonial style during this period,
but were, like those of the Midwest,
more rustic in appearance.
The Tudor-style gable is a
particularly handsome addition
to this basically Romanesque form.
Photograph, P. Kent Fairbanks,
HABS, 1967;
drawing, C. W. Barrow, Jr.,
1967.

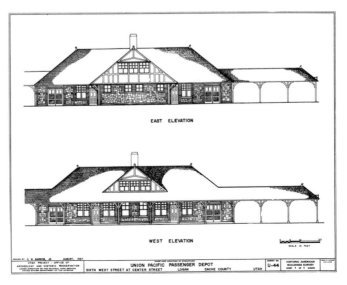

Feather River Inn Station,
Feather River Inn, California,
no known date.
*This was a stop, a flag stop to be sure,
on the Western Pacific's famed Feather River Canyon line.
There must have been many such log-cabin stations at one time,
perfect buildings to serve tourists "roughing it" in the wilderness.
The view dates from c. 1910.
Library of Congress.*

Many urban railroad stations of the mid-nineteenth century contained space for offices. The business of running a railroad, or even a branch line, required the services of many clerical employees, if not executives for personnel, freight, purchasing, operations, etc. As freight and passenger traffic increased, additional office space was usually met by building a new station or an addition to an old one. Every attempt was made to centralize the railroad's operations in at least one major building in each city. Most railroad companies occupied valuable property which was located in or near the center of the cities they served. By the end of the nineteenth century, given the rising value of urban real estate, they had to use this land more intensively.

The station/office building grew from this need. Starting with Philadelphia's Reading Terminal (1891-3), more and more struc-tures were erected which served not only passengers and company employees, but the business of outside firms and individuals. In time the station was to be almost submerged in the urban mass of commercial square feet. All that remains of Pennsylvania Station in New York, of course, are the tracks underlying the new Madison Square Garden. Grand Central Terminal in the same city has been overshadowed by the Pan Am Building, and, if champions of "progress" have their way, the famed façade and concourse will be leveled for yet another office building. It would all seem to make sense economically. Railroads are businesses, whether private or public, which must at least break even, if not show a paper profit. Many of the stations that remain, however, are now part of our cultural heritage. Ways to save them can and must be found.

Reading Terminal, Philadelphia, Pennsylvania, 1891-3.
F. H. Kimball and Wilson Brothers and Co.
were the architects of this building of Italian-Renaissance design.
The first three stories are faced in pink granite, and pink brick and terra cotta form the façade of the upper floors.
Railroad company offices for the Philadelphia and Reading were located in the upper levels.
Below the massive train shed to the rear, at street level, is the famed Farmer's Market,
one of the few left in operation in the central area of a major American city.
The railroad is now part of the Conrail system, and most of the office space has been abandoned.
The view dates from 1893. Dillon and Co., HABS.

Union Station (Pennsylvania Station),
Pittsburgh, Pennsylvania, 1898-1901, 1903.
A twelve-story office building and carriage concourse were designed by Daniel H. Burnham
to serve Pittsburgh's main railroad line, the Pennsylvania.
The single-span shed, designed by railroad engineers, was added two years later.
It was the last such span to be built in this country and has since been demolished.
The main building remains as a most evocative reminder of the railroad's last great days.
The rotunda, seen in a photograph and in a drawing,
is a beautifully conceived and worked Beaux-Arts structure.
The exterior photograph dates from 1921.
Rotunda photograph, Jack E. Boucher, HABS, 1963;
drawing, Carnegie Institute of Technology, HABS, 1963,

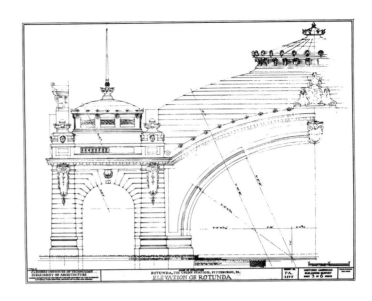

The Rotunda

Union Terminal, Terminal Tower, Cleveland, Ohio, 1923-1930,
*The Terminal Tower, designed by Graham, Anderson, Probst, and White, is still
one of the distinguishing landmarks of Cleveland and is located on the central Public Square.
Long-distance trains no longer use the building, but it is, at least,
still a center for what remains of Cleveland's rapid transit system.
The Van Sweringen brothers, developers of The Terminal Tower group of buildings, Shaker Heights,
and other important parcels of Cleveland-area real estate,
once saw the station as being the hub of a great transportation universe.
Presidents of nearly all the American railroads attended
the dedication ceremonies for the new building in 1930.
The 52-story, 708-feet-high tower,
was once the tallest skyscraper west of New York City.
Dudley Brumbach, 1961.*

It is fitting that the last significant and most monumental period of railroad station architecture in America should be its most classical. In the first years of the railroad, Greek Revival was considered the proper style for important buildings used by the public. Now, following the years of the Chicago's World Fair of 1893 until World War I, taste in design had come full circle. The clock tower which had first been raised in the Italianate style was projected even further in the Gothic and Romanesque; now it was subsumed in the mass of the classical palace. A horizontal form which grew progressively more and more vertical once again returned to a fairly level plane.

This was not, however, merely a revival of the Greek Revival. The style first articulated by Daniel Burnham and his partner Charles Atwood was based on Renaissance designs of mixed European origins. The arch, colonnade, dome, and column were projected in a monumental manner, as imperial, triumphal structural elements. They were not tucked into the façade *in antis,* but rather flaunted in a dramatic—even pompous—manner. In the best of these buildings—Washington's Union Station, New York's Pennsylvania and Grand Central stations—the effect was not, however, silly, but sublime. These were not mere flimsy movie sets ordered by Cecil B. de Mille. Carroll L. V. Meeks has explained it best:

> The colossal scale, ample sites, and vast interiors resulted from deliberate choices. Architects and corporations, influenced by the ideal of the City Beautiful, wished to contribute splendid, monumental structures to the urban scene. They were perfectly aware that they were subordinating economy and convenience to other values; but they held these other values to be of more lasting significance. The designers accepted as valid the classic conception that public buildings should be supremely impressive.

Now, in the age of artificial building materials, fourteen years after the destruction of Pennsylvania Station, we know that they were right.

World's Fair Terminal, Chicago, Illinois, 1893.
A temporary building, this was most certainly designed by Burnham's partner, Charles Atwood.
It was derived from the plan of a Roman bath
with monumental Corinthian columns framing three arched portals.
Library of Congress.

Union Station, Columbus, Ohio, 1897.
Daniel Burnham designed a central railroad building for Ohio's capital city.
In this view taken in 1919, the two grand arched portals and linking colonnade at street side
clearly define the station which lies behind them.
Library of Congress.

Union Station,
Washington, D. C., 1903-7.
Washington's great Burnham station has survived the urban warfare of the twentieth century. Some find its recently refurbished interior somewhat of a cosmic joke; the classically severe waiting room has been fitted out with something resembling a visual "conversation pit." But the basic structural integrity of the exterior and interior spaces have not been manhandled. The building now serves as the National Visitors' Center, and new facilities for Conrail's Amtrak trains are being built behind the old station. Jack E. Boucher, HABS, 1975.

Waiting room and arcade, Union Station.
*The great barrel-vaulted ceiling of the station is here perfectly captured.
Both this space and that of the exterior arcades give dignity and drama to even the most pedestrian activities of the traveler.
The waiting room photograph dates from 1915.
Waiting room, Baltimore and Ohio Railroad; arcade, Jack E. Boucher, HABS, 1968.*

STATION *in* NEW YORK CITY

TRAIN PLATFORMS - CONCOURSE ABOVE

Pennsylvania Station,
New York, New York, 1906-10.
Four years in creation,
McKim, Mead and White's
Penn Station also took
four years to wreck.
A great marble palace,
it boasted a train concourse of
indescribable structural beauty.
The aerial view and sketch date from 1910.
Pennsylvania Railroad.

Waiting room, Pennsylvania Station.
The grand staircase was
indeed something to descend.
The design of the great vaulted hall
was based on the Baths of Caracalla
and was no less splendid.
Cervin Robinson, HABS, 1962.

Street floor plan, Pennsylvania Station.
The extremely functional layout
of the building is clearly delineated here.
Passengers could enter and depart
on all sides of the building
or make direct underground connections
with the city's subway system.
The plan was drawn in 1910.
Pennsylvania Railroad.

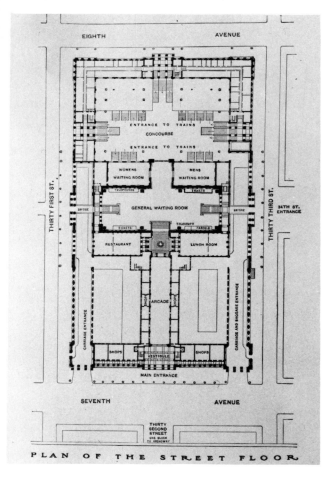

Concourse, Pennsylvania Station.

The soaring concourse of delicate glass and steel tracery, reaching up 150 feet,
never failed to impress visitors from abroad or, for that matter,
the many thousands of commuters who rushed to the platforms below.
Cervin Robinson HABS, 1962.

Façade sculpture, Grand Central Terminal, New York, New York, 1903-13.
*Seen in juxtaposition with the relentlessly monotonous Pan Am building, the south façade of
Grand Central and its sculptured pediment symbolize all that was good and glorious in the Beaux Arts tradition.
The building was begun by the firm of Reed and Stem and completed by Warren and Wetmore.
Plans to piggyback a 59-story office building on the structure now threaten this monument to enlightened railroad capitalism.*
Eric Schweikardt.

Broad Street Station,
Richmond, Virginia, 1917-19.
*John Russell Pope designed this neo-classical edifice for the Virginia state capital.
It was an appropriate monument for a region noted for its
pure Jeffersonian aesthetic in architecture.
H. H. Harwood, Jr., 1972.*

Union Station,
Tacoma, Washington, 1910.
*The dome of this building designed by Charles Reed and Allen Stem
rests on the intersection of four barrel vaults, and each of these ends in a monumental French arch.
It almost seems a pity that the architects felt it necessary to attach two side wings
of a nondescript style.
City of Tacoma.*

Pittsburgh and Lake Erie Railroad Terminal,
Pittsburgh, Pennsylvania, 1901.
*A relatively minor line, this railroad nevertheless needed an impressive Beaux-Arts station for its passengers.
The handsomely appointed waiting room boasts a splendid vaulted ceiling,
stained glass panels, and mahogany woodwork.
The station, which continues to function, is being restored
as part of the Station Square project of shops and a hotel.
Arthur Ziegler, HABS, 1974.*

Union Station,
Chicago, Illinois, 1916-25.
*Burnham first proposed a design for this station serving four major lines,
and this was revised after his death by the successor firm of Graham, Anderson, Probst, and White.
The handsome concourse was set off separately from a second block containing waiting rooms and offices.
Passengers boarded and departed from trains which ran under the concourse.
Philadelphia's 30th Street Station (1927-34), designed by the same firm,
is similarly situated along a riverfront and takes the same advantage of underground train platforms.
Chicago's concourse has been pulled to the ground.
Museum of History and Technology, Smithsonian Institution.*

In terms of architecture, the railroads have virtually paused to let the twentieth century pass by. Great classically-inspired temples were fashioned at the turn of the century until World War I, and, following this, Spanish-Colonial architects finished their work in the Mission Style. By the time of the Great Depression, the railroad companies were fat, rich, and tired. After struggling through the lean years of the 1930s, there was little or no energy or capital left to invest in innovative structures, in Creative Eclecticism. World War II represented a sort of respite. Gasoline was in short supply for automobiles, and there was freight to be moved to factories and piers. But within a few years of the war, the railroads were on the skids, and so were their stations. Only new management techniques and stringent curtailment of services saved some lines from bankruptcy. Most others had no choice but to surrender their real estate and rolling stock to publicly-funded authorities which, starting in the late 1960s, had been formed to offer an alternative to automobile pollution and congestion.

It is then a miracle that anything new and distinctive was produced in the "modern" style in the United States. The publicly-run lines of Europe and Canada were in somewhat better shape. Even during the Depression years extraordinarily inventive stations were built in Italy, France, Great Britain, and the Scandinavian countries. These were International Style structures, clean and streamlined. In more economically-advanced America, such an aesthetic was being applied to airport construction. The exceptions to this almost universally dismal scene in railroad architecture are to be found in scattered places throughout the United States—Omaha, Cincinnati, Buffalo, Burlington, Iowa. In some cases, a new railroad station was an absolute necessity. Cincinnati had to cope with a group of broken-down depots until 1933; the situation was similarly bad in Buffalo until the new station was built there in 1929. Fortunately, talented members of such architectural firms as Fellheimer and Wagner and Holabird and Root did not devote all their energies to the design of airline terminals and industrial plants.

Union Station, Omaha, Nebraska, 1929-30.
Omaha has long been a major American rail center and has shared with nearby Council Bluffs, Iowa, the distinction of being the common meeting ground for major Midwestern and Western railroads, including the Union Pacific, Rock Island, and Chicago and North Western. Designed by Gilbert S. Underwood, Union Station was ornamented in the popular Art-Déco fashion of the time, but remains a rather cold, inhospitable building. In many ways it is similar to other 1920s-'30s buildings, especially Newark, New Jersey's Pennsylvania Station erected five years later than the Omaha terminal. Although monumental in scale and interesting in ornamentation, these are curiously like mausoleums for the living dead. The view dates from 1938. Library of Congress.

Office, Chicago, Burlington and Quincy
Railroad, Denver, Colorado, 1938.
*The architectural firm of Holabird and Root
did much work for this innovative American
railroad line. Their stations in Burlington, Iowa
(1944), and La Crosse, Wisconsin (1944), are
graceful, functional buildings. The interior of the
C.B. & Q. office in Denver expresses almost
perfectly the contemporary, streamlined contours
of the railroad's famed Burlington Zephyr trains.
Private Collection.*

Long Island Railroad World's Fair Station,
New York, New York, 1939.
*Something very striking and original
was designed for the shuttle trains running from
Pennsylvania Station to Flushing Meadow,
Queens. The sweeping parabolic arch, already
familiar in Europe, is used here to functional and
aesthetic advantage. Private collection.*

Union Terminal, Cincinnati, Ohio, 1929-33,
Alfred Fellheimer and Steward Wagner.
*Successors to the firm of Reed and Stem, these architects understood and could articulate
the particular needs and the romance of modern rail transportation.
The single arched span is 200 feet in diameter and frames a combination waiting room and concourse.
It has been compared to a half-funnel feeding passengers to the platforms at the rear.
Its striking resemblance to the gently arched shape of radio receivers
and other domestic furnishings of the time has also been noted.
The terminal now stands empty, and hopefully some new use will be found for it.
New York Public Library.*

Most railroad stations left remaining in America will never again serve their original purpose. Rail transportation may make a comeback. It is considerably more energy efficient and pollution free than either automobile or air travel. For carrying passengers relatively short distances, only bus lines can hope to compete in strictly economic terms. If, as is to be hoped, roadbeds and equipment are steadily improved, then a new generation of Americans may live to see not· only the advantages but the real pleasure to be derived from rail transportation.

The stations are, for the most part, hopelessly dated and despoiled structures for modern-day use. The vastness of many urban terminals is sufficient argument for their abandonment. They are costly to heat and almost impossible to keep free from the excrescences of amateur artists, commercial and criminal. It is no wonder then that Conrail, the successor public corporation to six major lines in the Northeast, should choose to erect box-like sheds for new stations. At least, one can say, the trains are still running.

What then·to do with the old? Must these buildings be demolished? Some are now so squalid that only a bulldozer can effectively disinfect the site. But the majority, the vast majority, are worthy of salvation. There is no reason, outside of our lack of imagination and excess of greed, why they should not be "recycled" as community centers, art galleries, restaurants, inns, historical museums, visitors' centers, public libraries. Readers of *Waiting for the 5:05* are urged to read *Reusing Railroad Stations,* a report from Educational Facilities Laboratories and the National Endowment for the Arts (850 Third Avenue, New York, N.Y. 10022). This handsome paperback publication illustrates and documents how the idea of preserving railroad stations is working—in Duluth, Minnesota; Lincoln, Nebraska; Oberlin, Ohio; Hartford, Connecticut; to mention just a few of the towns and cities across the country. Even villages such as Plains, Georgia, have learned how to reuse their country depots. It could become a national drive.

The Mount Royal Station in Baltimore, Maryland, is one such building that has been saved from oblivion. It now serves as the home of the Maryland Institute of Arts. In 1964 Baltimore citizens raised $1,000,000 to help the Institute purchase and remodel the station. The proposed addition to New York's Metropolitan Museum, ironically, will cost at least twenty times that amount.

Waiting room and Library.
The suitability of reusing this space for the arts
is graphically illustrated in these two photographs.
Architect Richard Donkervoet imaginatively reworked the interior to make maximum use of the dramatic space.
The exterior was little changed, and every possible bit of architectural detailing was retained.
In all, 25,000 square feet of usable space were gained, and renovation costs,
at eighteen dollars per square foot, were considerably lower
than the twenty-five dollars per square foot for new construction.
Waiting room, Lanny Miyamote, HABS, 1958;
library, Robert M. Vogel, Smithsonian Institution, 1973.

(Opposite) Mount Royal Station, Baltimore, Maryland, 1894-5.
The photograph of the exterior was taken around 1900 and fully illustrates
the fine late-romantic lines of the station, designed by E. Francis Baldwin and Josias Pennington.
A Romanesque tower of fine proportions dominates the low-lying Italian Renaissance structure.
Even the decorative ironwork railings of the platforms
were executed with conspicuous taste.
Citizens were justifiably concerned about the fate of this Baltimore and Ohio station.
Exterior, Smithsonian Institution;
ironwork, William Edmund Barrett, HAER, 1971.

Canada's railway lines, both privately and publicly owned, have been interwoven with their American counterparts for well over one-hundred years. Two of the five companies which were merged after World War I to make up the Canadian National Railways—the Grand Trunk and Central Vermont railways—served primarily American towns and cities in New England, New York state, Michigan, Minnesota, and Washington state. The Canadian Pacific Railways has controlled and operated nearly 4,000 miles of lines in the United States. The stations built across Canada and in America by these various companies are similiar in many respects to those built south of its border at the same time by United States railroads.

The railroad is still a viable means of transportation in Canada, and the many well-appointed stations and hotels still remaining testify to the benefits of central planning and administration, if not public funding. "The most progressive station yet built on this continent," historian Carroll Meeks wrote in 1956, is the Montreal Central Station built for the Canadian National Railways. "It combines a maximum of directness and a minimum of pyrotechnics." The romantic Canadian Pacific hotels such as the Chateau Frontenac at Quebec City and the Chateau Lake Louise and Banff Springs in Alberta are further evidence of a continuing tradition of thoughtful and enterprising service to the public.

Windsor Station, Montreal, Quebec, 1888.
*This has served the Canadian Pacific Railway Company
as its main station and headquarters building
since the late nineteenth century.
The original structure was comprised of only
the seven-story section to the left.
This was considerably remodeled in 1911-12
when the addition was made.
An accounting office wing was added at the far left in 1954.
Bruce Price, a New York architect, designed
the original building in the Richardsonian manner.
He was also the architect
of a later station at the Place Viger.
Canadian Pacific.*

Bonaventure Station, Montreal, Quebec, late nineteenth century.
The Grand Trunk Railway offered its passengers a truly splendid waiting room;
it was in every sense "1st Class" as the etched glass fan light, at right, proclaims.
Canadian National Railways.

Central Station, Montreal, Quebec, 1938-43.
Work on this station was begun in 1931 and later resumed under the direction of architect John Schofield.
It is somewhat of a wonder that it was completed in the midst of World War II.
Now, as originally planned, the air rights have been developed, and the Queen Elizabeth Hotel rises above
the station. Although a handsome station has been completely submerged, the street-level concourse
and below-ground platforms have been retained in a functional and an accommodating manner.
Canadian National Railways.

Union Station, Toronto, Ontario, 1914-27.
This monumental Beaux-Arts building was intended to serve the Grand Trunk and Canadian National systems.
The main façade is 720 feet in length and is imperially defined by twenty-one Doric columns.
Ross and McDonald, Hugh G. Jones, and John M. Lyle served as the architects.
Canadian National Railways.

MacDonald Hotel, Edmonton, Alberta, late nineteenth century.
The new and the old have been effectively combined in this Canadian National Railways hotel.
It is typical of the French-Renaissance style buildings erected at important points
along both the Canadian National and Canadian Pacific lines.
Canadian National Railways.